CHRISTMAS COOKIES RECIPES

Enjoy Holiday Cooking Quick & Easy Cookies Cookbook

(Let This Christmas Recipes and Also the Tastiest in All Time)

Gilbert Arnold

Published by Alex Howard

© **Gilbert Arnold**

All Rights Reserved

Christmas Cookies Recipes: Enjoy Holiday Cooking Quick & Easy Cookies Cookbook (Let This Christmas Recipes and Also the Tastiest in All Time)

ISBN 978-1-990169-48-9

All rights reserved. No part of this guide may be reproduced in any form without permission in writing from the publisher except in the case of brief quotations embodied in critical articles or reviews.

Legal & Disclaimer

The information contained in this book is not designed to replace or take the place of any form of medicine or professional medical advice. The information in this book has been provided for educational and entertainment purposes only.

The information contained in this book has been compiled from sources deemed reliable, and it is accurate to the best of the Author's knowledge; however, the Author cannot guarantee its accuracy and validity and cannot be held liable for any errors or omissions. Changes are periodically made to this book. You must consult your doctor or get professional medical advice before using any of the suggested remedies, techniques, or information in this book.

Table of contents

PART 1 1

INTRODUCTION 2

Brilliant Black And White Chocolate Dipped Shortbread Cookies 3
Santas Favourite Super Soft Chocolate Chip Cookies 4
Amazing Gingerbread Cookies 5
4 Ingredinent Festive Fudge Crinkles 7
3 Ingredient Peanut Butter Cookies 8
Awesome Almond Spritz Press Cookies 9
Super Snowball Cookies 10
Delicious Butter Cookies 11
Russian Tea Cake Cookies 12
Christmas Coconut Macaroons 13
Cinnamon Cookies 14
Winter Wonderland Cranberry Oatmeal Cookies 15
Perfect Pecan Bourbon Balls 16
Magical Mint Cookies 17
Apricot And Almond Cookies 19
Cheerful Chocolate And Cherry Cookies 20
Chai Spiced Sugar Cookies 21
Classic Gingersnap Cookies 23
Excellent Expresso Cookies 25
Rad Red Velvet Brownies 26
Mandelspritzgebäck 28
Eggnog Cookies 29
Lemon Love Cookies 31
Mesmirizing Meringue Cookies 32
Delicious Dark Chocolate Walnut Cookies 33
Stained Glass Windows Cookies 35
Raspberry Swirl Surprise Cookies 37
Great Griscotti 39
Easy Peezy Pumpkin Cookies 41
Happy Honey Hazelnut Cookies 42

DELICIOUS PALEO CHRISTMAS RECIPES 43

Drinks 43
Yule-Time Pumpkin Latte 43
Santa's Sangria 44
Paleo Eggnog 45
Creamy Christmas Cider 46
Cranberry Christmas Cocktail 47

STARTERS 48

Paleo Holiday Starters 48
Beef And Bacon Balls 49
Paleo Pinwheel Bites 50
Egg Cups 51
Garlic And Almond Thins 52
Macadamia And Cashew Cream And Crackers 53
Holiday Spiced Nuts 54
Bacon And Sweet Potato Casserole 55

SALADS AND SIDE DISHES 56

Asparagus Wrapped In Proscuitto 56
Holiday Paleo Buns 57
Green Casserole 58
Christmas Fauxtatoes 59

RED AND GREEN PALEO SALAD 60

ENTREES 61

Herb Crusted Roasted Lamb 61
Savory Cinnamon Pork 62
Salmon In Saffron 63
Herb Roasted Turkey Breast 64
Bacon And Wild Mushroom Steaks 65
Stuffed Pork Chops 66
Stuffed Squash 67

DESSERTS 68

Choco Almond Bites 68
Mint Chocolate Squares 69
Macadamia Apple Crispies 70
Chocolate Cream Cups 71
Slow Cooked Apple Pecan Crisp 72

CHRISTMAS CASSEROLE RECIPES 73

Christmas Morning Casserole 73
Herbed Bacon And Mushroom Casserole 74
Baked Christmas Brunch Casserole 75
Red And Green Holiday Casserole 76
Creamy Artichoke Casserole 77
Buttered Salmon And Croissant Casserole 78
Make-Ahead Christmas Casserole 79
Leftover Holiday Ham And Potato Casserole 80
Savory French Toast Bakes 81
Creamed Onion Casserole 82
Garlic Cheddar Potato Casserole 83
Creamy Baked Oyster Casserole 84
Leftover Turkey And Potato Casserole 85
Broccoli And Cheesy Rice Casserole 86
Eggnog And Sweet Potato Casserole 87
Creamed Corn Casserole 88
Turkey And Mashed Potato Casserole 89
Creamy Green Bean Casserole 90
Baked Overnight Eggnog 91
Creamy Layered Potatoes 92

PART 2 93

Antipasto Cups 94
The Best Homemade Low Carb Keto Eggnog Velvety Smooth 96
Bacon Collard Greens 98
Christmas Cauliflower Casserole 100
Creamy Parmesan Spinach Bake 102
Garlic Roasted Broccoli 104
Cauliflower Au Gratin Gluten Free 106

CRISPY BRUSSELS SPROUTS WITH PANCETTA	108
KETO STUFFING RECIPE	110
ROASTED BROCCOLI AND CAULIFLOWER RECIPE WITH PARMESAN GARLIC LOW CARB GLUTENFREE	112
SOUTHERNSTYLE GREEN BEANS	114
SUGAR FREE GINGERBREAD MEN	116
SUGAR FREE WALNUT AND BRANDY TRUFFLES	118
CHICKEN MOLE	120
CLASSIC GINGERBREAD MEN LOW CARB AND GLUTEN FREE	122
FOUR INGREDIENT FLOURLESS SUGAR FREE PISTACHIO COOKIES	124
GLUTENFREE LOW CARB PEANUT BUTTER COOKIES MADE WITH SIX INGREDIENTS	126
HOLIDAY PRALINE NO BAKE COOKIES THMS LOW CARB SUGAR FREE	128
LOW CARB PEANUT BUTTER BLOSSOMS	130
PEANUT BUTTER CHOCOLATE CHIP COOKIES THMS LOW CARB SUGAR FREE	132
SUGAR FREE PALEO PECAN SNOWBALL COOKIES	134
CRANBERRY GLAZED HAM LOW CARB AND GLUTEN FREE	136
HAM GRUYERE MINI QUICHES	138
BAKED PARMESAN ZUCCHINI ROUNDS	140
BUTTERY CAULIFLOWER RICE PILAF LOW CARB GLUTEN FREE	141
LOW CARB LEMON CHEESECAKE BARS	143
NO CARB PEANUT BUTTER COOKIES	145
ROSEMARY MUSTARD CRUSTED BAKED HAM LOW CARB GLUTEN FREE	146
KETO PUMPKIN BUTTER COOKIES RECIPE	147
BETTER THAN POTATOES CHEESY CAULIFLOWER PUREE LOW CARB	149
LOW CARB AVGOLEMENO GREEK CHICKEN LEMON EGG SOUP	151
LOW CARB BUFFALO CHICKEN MEATBALLS	153
LOW CARB CHEESE CRACKERS RECIPE KETO FRIENDLY	155
LOW CARB PUMPKIN CHEESECAKE MOUSSE	157
OVEN ROASTED GREEN BEANS	159
PARMESAN ROASTED TOMATOES RECIPE	160
KETO BROWNIES WITH PEPPERMINT CRUNCH	162
SPICY BROCCOLI WITH GARLIC	164
LOW CARB WHITE CHOCOLATE COCONUT FUDGE PALEO KETO	165
CRANBERRY ORANGE CARDAMOM GLAZE	167
SPICY MOLASSES COOKIES GLUTEN FREE REFINED SUGARFREE	168

PUMPKIN PIE SNOWBALL COOKIES 170
CHOCOLATE GINGERBREAD MEN GRAIN FREE 172
KETO HAM MAPLE GLAZED 176
LOW CARB CHRISTMAS TREE PLATTER 178
LOW CARB CRANBERRY SAUCE 180
GERMAN CINNAMON STARS LOW CARB CHRISTMAS COOKIES 182
THE BEST LOWCARB TORTILLA CHIPS 184
LOW CARB CINNAMON CHIPS 186
LOW CARB COCOA NUTS 187

Part 1

Introduction

It's the most magical time of year and what better way to indulge in festive cheer than with homemade, Christmas cookies! Delicious, sweet and bursting with seasonal joy, these gorgeous cookie creations will fill your senses with Christmas flavours. Experiment with these recipes in the Winter months and soon you will discover your personal Christmas biscuit favourites! You'll have to wait and see which one Santa likes the best though!
So throw on the Christmas playlist, pour yourself your favourite seasonal bevergae and lets get baking!

Brilliant Black And White Chocolate Dipped Shortbread Cookies

INGREDIENTS:
Ingredients
1 cup flour
1/4 cup sugar
1 teaspoon vanilla extract
1/2 teaspoon orange zest
Pinch salt
8 tablespoons (1 stick) unsalted butter, cold, chunked
2 cups chopped dark chocolate

DIRECTIONS:

Firstly, mix the flour, sugar, vanilla extract, orange zest and salt in a food processor; pulse to lightly mix. Next, add the butter and pulse until combined. Form the dough into a disk and wrap in plastic. Allow to chill for 30 minutes.

Meanwhile preheat the oven to 350 degrees F.

On a lightly floured work surface, roll the cookie dough out to a 1/4-inch thickness. Cut out cookies using a 1 1/2-inch round cutter. Arrange the cookies, spaced at least 1-inch apart, on a parchment-lined baking sheet.

Bake until the cookies are a nice yet pale golden brown colur, this should take about 15 minutes. Remember to rotate halfway through. Let them cool slightly, then transfer the cookies to a wire rack to cool completely.

Heat an inch of water in a small saucepot. Place the chocolate in a heatproof bowl and set it over the saucepot Bring the water to a simmer. When the chocolate has melted, immediately remove the bowl from the saucepot and whisk the chocolate until smooth. Dip the cookies halfway into the chocolate and place them on parchment paper to set. Once the chocolate has set, enjoy.

Santas Favourite Super Soft Chocolate Chip Cookies

INGREDIENTS:
- 2 1/4cups flour
- 1teaspoon baking soda
- 3/4cup packed brown sugar
- 1/2cup butter, softened
- 1/2cup shortening
- 1/4cup sugar
- 1(4 ounce) package instant vanilla pudding
- 1teaspoon vanilla extract
- 1/8teaspoon almond extract
- 2 eggs, beaten
- 2 cups chocolate chips

DIRECTIONS:

1. Preheat oven 350 degrees.
2. Combine flour and baking soda.
3. In a large bowl beat brown sugar, sugar, butter, shortening, pudding mix, vanilla, and almond extract.
4. Mix until well blended.
5. Add eggs and mix well.
6. Beat in the flour mixture.
7. Stir in chocolate chips.
8. Drop by rounded teaspOonful and bake 10-12 minutes.

Amazing Gingerbread Cookies

INGREDIENTS:
1. 2 cups all-purpose flour (spooned and leveled), plus more for rolling
2. 2 teaspoons ground ginger
3. 1 teaspoon ground cinnamon
4. 1/2 teaspoon ground nutmeg
5. 1/4 teaspoon ground cloves
6. 1/4 teaspoon baking soda
7. 1/4 teaspoon salt
8. 1/2 cup (1 stick) unsalted butter, room temperature
9. 1/3 cup packed dark-brown sugar
10. 1/3 cup unsulfured molasses
11. 1 large egg
12. Decorating sugar or sprinkles (optional)

DIRECTIONS:

1. In a medium bowl, whisk together flour, spices, baking soda, and salt; set aside. With an electric mixer, beat butter and brown sugar until smooth. Beat in molasses and egg. With mixer on low, add dry ingredients; mix just until a dough forms. Place dough on floured plastic wrap; pat into an 8-inch square. Wrap well; chill until firm, 1 to 2 hours.
2. Preheat oven to 350 degrees. Divide dough in half.

3.Working with one half at a time (rewrap and refrigerate other half), place dough on floured parchment or waxed paper; roll out 1/8 inch thick, turning, lifting, and flouring dough (and rolling pin) as needed. Freeze dough (on paper) until firm, about 20 minutes.

4.Loosen dough from paper. Cut out shapes, and transfer to baking sheets. Decorate with sugar or sprinkles, as desired.

5.Bake until firm and edges just begin to darken, 10 to 18 minutes, depending on size. Cool completely on baking sheets.

4 Ingredinent Festive Fudge Crinkles

INGREDIENTS:
- (18 1/4 ounce) box devil's food cake mix (Betty Crocker Super Moist suggested)
- 1⁄2cup vegetable oil
- 2large eggs
- granulated sugar for rolling

DIRECTIONS:

1. Begin by stirring by hand the dry cake mix, oil and eggs in a large bowl until a dough consistency forms.
2. Dust your hands with confectioners' sugar and shape dough into 1" balls.
3. Roll balls in confectioners' sugar and place 2 inches apart on ungreased cookie sheets.
4. Bake for 8-10 minutes or until center is JUST SET.
5. Remove from pans after a minute or so and cool on wire racks.

3 Ingredient Peanut Butter Cookies

INGREDIENTS:
- 1 cup peanut butter
- 1 cup sugar
- 1 egg

DIRECTIONS:

1. Preheat oven to 350 degrees.
2. Combine all ingredients in a bowl.
3. Mix until well combined.
4. Form into 1" balls.
5. Bake at 350 until golden brown.
6. To make more than 1 run of cookies simply double the recipe

Awesome Almond Spritz Press Cookies

INGREDIENTS:
- 1 cup shortening
- 3/4 cup sugar
- 1 egg
- 2 1/4 cups sifted flour
- 1/8 teaspoon salt
- 1/4 teaspoon baking powder
- 1 teaspoon almond extract
- food coloring

DIRECTIONS:

1. Cream the shortening and add the sugar in gradually.
2. Then add unbeaten egg, sifted dry ingredients, flavoring and a few drops of food coloring. Mix well.
3. Fill cookie press. Form the cookies on ungreased cookie sheets using a tree plate. Decorate with tiny multi-colored sprinkles.
4. Bake at 400°F for 6-8 minutes. Cool just slightly and remove from cookie sheet to cooling rack.

Super Snowball Cookies

INGREDIENTS:
- ½ cup butter
- 2 tablespoons sugar
- 1 teaspoon vanilla
- 3⁄4 cup chopped pecans
- 1 cup flour
- 1/4 teaspoon salt
- powdered sugar, reserved

DIRECTIONS:

1. Cream butter until light.
2. Add all other ingredients, except the powdered sugar.
3. Mix well.
4. Shape into 1" balls and place on a greased cookie sheet.
5. Bake at 350 degrees 15 minutes.
6. These should be nice and pale in colour so be sure not to brown them. Cool and roll in powdered sugar.

Delicious Butter Cookies

INGREDIENTS:
- 8 ounces unsalted butter
- 3/4 cup granulated sugar
- 1/4 teaspoon salt
- 1 1/2 teaspoons pure vanilla extract
- 1 large egg yolk
- 2 cups all purpose flour

DIRECTIONS:

1. First, beat the butter, sugar, salt and vanilla together well until you have a smooth and creamy mixture
2. Next, mix in the egg yolk until well incorporated, scraping down the sides of the bowl a few times.
3. Add the flour and mix just until incorporated.
4. Scrape onto a lightly floured board and knead a few times, just until the dough smooths out.
5. Turn onto a sheet of plastic wrap and roll into a log, wrap up and refrigerate for several hours or freeze.
6. Before baking, preheat the oven to 325°F.
7. Line your baking sheets with parchment.
8. Slice the dough into slices about 1/8" thick and place them on the sheets about an inch apart
9. Bake until JUST beginning to turn golden around the edges, about 16-18 minutes.

Russian Tea Cake Cookies

INGREDIENTS:
- 1 cup butter or 1 cup margarine, softened
- 1/2 cup powdered sugar
- 1 teaspoon vanilla
- 2 1/4 cups all purpose flour
- 1/4 teaspoon salt
- 3/4 cup finely chopped nuts
- powdered sugar

DIRECTIONS:

1. Pre Heat oven to 400 degrees F.
2. Beat the butter, 1/2 cup powdered sugar and the vanilla in large bowl with electric mixer on medium speed, or you can simply mix with spoon.
3. Stir in the flour and salt.
4. Stir in the nuts.
5. Shape the dough into 1-inch balls.
6. Place about 2 inches apart on ungreased cookie sheet.
7. Bake 8 to 9 minutes or until set but not brown.
8. Immediately remove from cookie sheet; roll in powdered sugar.
9. Cool completely on wire rack.
10. Roll in powdered sugar again.

Christmas Coconut Macaroons

INGREDIENTS:
- 14 ounces sweetened coconut flakes
- 14 ounces sweetened condensed milk
- 1 teaspoon pure vanilla extract
- 2 extra large egg whites, at room temperature
- 1/4 teaspoon kosher salt

DIRECTIONS:

1. Preheat your oven to 325 degrees F.
2. Combine the coconut, condensed milk, and vanilla in a large bowl.
3. Whip the egg whites and salt on high speed in the bowl of an electric mixer fitted with the whisk attachment until they make medium-firm peaks.
4. Gently fold the egg whites into the coconut mixture.
5. Drop the batter onto sheet pans lined with parchment paper using either a 1 3/4-inch diameter ice cream scoop, or 2 teaspoons.
6. Bake for 25 to 30 minutes, until golden brown.
7. Allow to cool on wire racks.

Cinnamon Cookies

INGREDIENTS:

for the cookies

1. 200 grams butter
2. 200 grams sugar
3. 2 tablespoons golden syrup
4. 300 grams flour
5. 3 teaspoons cinnamon
6. 1 teaspoon bicarbonate of soda

for the topping

1. nuts
2. cinnamon
3. sugar

DIRECTIONS:

1. Mix butter and sugar. Add the rest of the ingredients except the "topping".
2. Roll the dough and make small "sausages" as long as the baking tray, three on each tray, and push them flat with your fingers...
3. Top them with 1 decilitre chopped almonds or hazelnuts or a mix of the two, extra cinnamon and sugar. bake 175-200 Celsius for 10-15 minutes. They are soft and good right after you take them out of the oven, but even better when they have cooled down and crispy.

Winter Wonderland Cranberry Oatmeal Cookies

INGREDIENTS:
- 3/4 cup sugar
- 1/4 cup packed brown sugar
- 1/2 cup butter, softened
- 1 large egg
- 1/2 teaspoon vanilla extract
- 1/2 teaspoon cinnamon
- 1/2 teaspoon baking soda
- 1/4 teaspoon salt
- 1 cup all purpose flour
- 1 1/2 cups quick cooking oats
- 3/4 cup dried cranberries
- 6 ounces white chocolate chips

DIRECTIONS:

1. Firstly preheat oven to 375°F.
2. Next, in a large bowl using an electric mixer combine the sugar, brown sugar and butter; mix well till creamed.
3. Add in egg and vanilla extract and mix until combined.
4. Add the cinnamon, baking soda, salt and flour and mix well.
5. Fold in the oatmeal, dried cranberries and white chocolate chips- making sure that all ingredients are uniformly distributed.
6. Roll dough into 1-inch balls and place 3 inches apart onto a greased cookie sheet and bake at 375° for 10-12 minutes, just until the edges are lightly golden.
7. Remove from oven and let cool for 2-3 minutes on the cookie sheet, then transfer cookies to cooling rack.

Perfect Pecan Bourbon Balls

INGREDIENTS:

1 (12-oz.) package vanilla wafers, finely crushed

1 cup powdered sugar

1 cup finely chopped toasted pecans

1/2 cup bourbon

2 tablespoons unsweetened cocoa

2 tablespoons light corn syrup

Powdered sugar

Buttey toasted pecans, coarsley chopped

DIRECTIONS:

1. Stir together first 6 ingredients. Shape into 1-inch balls. Roll in powdered sugar or pecans. Refrigerate up to 2 weeks.

Magical Mint Cookies

INGREDINETS:

3 cups all-purpose flour

1 1/3 cups unsweetened cocoa

1/2 teaspoon table salt

1 cup butter, softened

1 cup granulated sugar

1/2 cup firmly packed light brown sugar

1 tablespoon instant coffee granules

2 teaspoons vanilla extract

1/2 teaspoon peppermint extract

2 large eggs

PARCHMENT PAPER

1 cup crushed hard peppermint candies

DIRECTIONS:

1. Stir together flour and next 2 ingredients. Beat butter and next 5 ingredients at medium speed with an electric mixer 3 to 4 minutes or until creamy. Add eggs, and beat until smooth. Add flour mixture, and beat just until blended.
2. Divide dough into 2 equal portions. Flatten into disks between parchment paper. Roll each to 1/4-inch thickness; transfer to a baking sheet, and chill 30 minutes.
3. Preheat oven to 350°. Place 1 dough disk on work surface, and remove top sheet of parchment paper. Cut with a lightly floured 2 1/2-inch round cutter, rerolling scraps once; place 1 inch apart on 2 parchment paper-lined baking sheets.
4. Sprinkle 1 tsp. crushed peppermint candies onto each cookie. Repeat procedure with remaining dough and candy.
5. Bake at 350° for 12 minutes or until firm. Transfer cookies to a wire rack, and cool.

Apricot And Almond Cookies

INGREDIENTS:

2 cups butter, softened

2/3 cup granulated sugar

2/3 cup firmly packed light brown sugar

1 teaspoon almond extract

1/4 teaspoon kosher salt

4 2/3 cups all-purpose flour

1 1/2 cups chopped sliced almonds

PARCHMENT PAPER

3/4 cup apricot preserves

DIRECTIONS:

1. Beat first 5 ingredients at medium speed with an electric mixer 3 to 5 minutes or until creamy. Add flour; beat just until blended.

2. Shape dough into 1-inch balls (about 1 Tbsp. per ball), and roll in almonds. Place 2 inches apart on 2 parchment paper lined-baking sheets. Press thumb or end of a wooden spoon into each ball, forming an indentation. Chill 20 minutes.

3. Preheat oven to 350°. Bake 15 minutes or until bottoms are light golden brown. Cool on baking sheets 10 minutes; transfer to wire racks, and cool 10 minutes. Spoon 1/2 tsp. apricot preserves into each indentation.

Cheerful Chocolate And Cherry Cookies

INGREDIENTS:
- 1 cup shortening
- 1 1/2 cups white sugar
- 2 large eggs
- 1 teaspoon almond extract
- 2 cups flour
- 1 teaspoon baking powder
- 1/4 teaspoon salt
- 1 cup semi-sweet chocolate chips
- 1 1/2 cups coconut
- 1 1/2 cups chopped marashino cherries

DIRECTIONS:

1. Cream shortening and sugar in large bowl with electric mixer until well blended.
2. Add eggs and almond extract, beating on medium speed until light and fluffy; about 2 minutes.
3. Combine flour, baking powder and salt. Add to creamed mixture gradually, beating on low speed just until blended. Fold in chips, coconut and cherries.
4. Drop dough by spoonfuls onto greased cookie sheets.
5. Bake at 350° for 12-15 minutes or until lightly browned around edges.

Chai Spiced Sugar Cookies

INGREDIENTS:
1. 2 3/4 cups all-purpose flour
2. 1 teaspoon baking soda
3. 1/2 teaspoon baking powder
4. 1/2 teaspoon salt
5. 1 3/4 cups white sugar
6. 2 1/2 teaspoons ground cinnamon
7. 1 teaspoon ground ginger
8. 1 teaspoon ground cardamom
9. 1/2 teaspoon ground allspice
10. 1/4 teaspoon finely ground black pepper
11. 1 cup unsalted butter, softened
12. 1 egg
13. 1/2 teaspoon vanilla extract

DIRECTIONS:

1. Preheat oven to 350 degrees. Line a baking sheet with parchment paper; set aside.
2. In a large bowl, sift together flour, baking soda, baking powder and salt. Set aside.
3. In a medium bowl combine sugar, cinnamon, ginger, cardamom, allspice and black pepper. Remove 1/4 cup of the sugar-spice mixture, set aside to reserve for rolling the cookies.
4. In the bowl of a stand mixer fitted with the paddle attachment or in a large bowl with an electric mixer, beat the butter and sugar-spice mixture until light and fluffy, about 3 minutes.
5. Beat in egg and vanilla extract, combine until fully incorporated.
6. Slowly blend in dry ingredients mixing until just combined.
7. Using a small scoop (2 teaspoons) roll dough into balls and then into the reserved sugar-spice mixture. Place dough balls on prepared baking sheet about 1 1/2 inches apart.
8. Bake in preheated oven for 8 to 10 minutes.
9. Let stand on baking sheet two minutes before removing to cool on wire racks.

Classic Gingersnap Cookies

INGREDIENTS:
3½ cups all-purpose flour
2¼ teaspoons baking soda
1 teaspoon salt
1¼ teaspoons cinnamon
1¼ teaspoons ground cloves
1 teaspoon ground ginger
1 cup unsalted butter, at room temperature
1 cup granulated sugar
½ cup molasses
2 tablespoons vegetable oil
2 eggs
1 teaspoon vanilla extract

DIRECTIONS:
1. Preheat oven to 350 degrees F. Line two baking sheets with parchment paper; set aside.
2. In a medium bowl, whisk together the flour, baking soda, salt, cinnamon, cloves and ginger; set aside.
3. Using an electric mixer, cream together the butter and sugar on medium speed until light and fluffy, about 3 minutes. Add the molasses and continue to mix until completely combined, scraping the sides of the bowl as needed. Add the vegetable oil, eggs and vanilla extract, and mix to thoroughly combine. Scrape the sides of the bowl, reduce the mixer speed to low, and add the flour mixture. Mix until just combined, giving it a final stir with a rubber spatula.
4. Scoop about 1½ tablespoons of dough, roll into a ball, and place on prepared baking sheets about 2 inches apart. Bake for 10 to 12 minutes, or until edges are set, but centers are still soft. Allow the cookies to sit on the baking sheets for 5 minutes, then transfer to a wire rack to cool completely. The cookies can be

kept in an airtight container at room temperature for up to 1 week. These cookies can also be frozen for up to 1 month.

Excellent Expresso Cookies

INGREDIENTS:

1 cup butter, softened

1/2 cup granulated sugar

1 teaspoon sea salt

1 teaspoon vanilla extract

2 cups all-purpose flour

1/2 cup chocolate-covered espresso beans, chopped

1 tablespoon finely ground espresso beans

Wax paper

1/2 cup Demerara or turbinado sugar, divided

DIRECTIONS:
1. Beat first 3 ingredients at medium speed with a electric stand mixer 2 to 3 minutes or until light and fluffy. Stir in vanilla.
2. Stir together flour and next 2 ingredients in a medium bowl. Gradually add to butter mixture, beating just until blended; stop to scrape bowl as needed.3. Divide dough in half. Turn 1 dough portion out onto wax paper, and shape into a 10- x 2-inch log. Sprinkle log with 3 Tbsp. Demerara sugar, and roll log back and forth to adhere. Repeat with remaining dough portion and 3 Tbsp. Demerara sugar. Wrap logs in plastic wrap, and chill 2 to 3 hours.
4. Preheat oven to 350°. Cut chilled dough into 1/4-inch-thick slices, and place 1 inch apart on 2 lightly greased baking sheets. Sprinkle 1 1/2 tsp. Demerara sugar over cookies on each sheet.
5. Bake, in batches, at 350° for 12 to 15 minutes or until golden around edges, switching baking sheets halfway through.
6. Transfer to wire racks; cool 5 minutes. Serve immediately, or cool completely.

Rad Red Velvet Brownies

INGREDIENTS:

1 (4-oz.) bittersweet chocolate baking bar, chopped

3/4 cup butter

2 cups sugar

4 large eggs

1 1/2 cups all-purpose flour

1 (1-oz.) bottle red liquid food coloring

1 1/2 teaspoons baking powder

1 teaspoon vanilla extract

1/8 teaspoon salt

Cream cheese frosting

Garnish: white chocolate curls

DIRECTIONS:

1. Preheat oven to 350°. Line bottom and sides of a 9-inch square pan with aluminum foil, allowing 2 to 3 inches to extend over sides; lightly grease foil.
2. Microwave chocolate and butter in a large microwave-safe bowl at HIGH 1 1/2 to 2 minutes or until melted and smooth, stirring at 30-second intervals. Whisk in sugar. Add eggs, 1 at a time, whisking just until blended after each addition. Gently stir in flour and next 4 ingredients. Pour mixture into prepared pan.

3. Bake at 350° for 44 to 48 minutes or until a wooden pick inserted in center comes out with a few moist crumbs. Cool completely on a wire rack (about 2 hours).

4. Lift brownies from pan, using foil sides as handles; gently remove foil. Spread Cheese Frosting on top of brownies, and cut into 16 squares. Garnish, if desired.

Mandelspritzgebäck

INGREDIENTS:
- 1 1/3 cups unsalted butter (softened)
- 1 1/4 cups sugar
- 1 large egg
- 1 large egg yolk
- 1 1/3 cups ground almonds (blanched)
- 3 drops bitter almond oil (see note)
- 4 cups all purpose flour
- 2 1/2 teaspoons baking powder

DIRECTIONS:

1. Grease baking trays.
2. Mix butter with sugar until creamy. Add egg and egg yolk and mix until foamy.
3. Add almonds and a few drops oil of bitter almonds.
4. Add flour (mixed with baking powder) little by little and mix. The dough should be elastic, but will not be smooth.
5. Fill in the dough into a cookie press with big star nozzle or better into a meat grinder with a big star nozzle.
6. Make/press dough strings of about 2 to 3-inches. Form dough strings into rings, "S", horseshoes or any other shapes you like and place on baking tray.
7. Bake for about 12 minutes. Cookies should still be light.

Eggnog Cookies

INGREDIENTS:
1. 2 1/4 cups all-purpose flour
2. 2 tsp baking powder
3. 1/2 tsp salt
4. 1/2 tsp ground nutmeg, plus more for topping
5. 1/2 tsp ground cinnamon
6. 3/4 cup unsalted butter, at room temperature
7. 1/2 cup granulated sugar
8. 1/2 cup packed light-brown sugar
9. 2 large egg yolks
10. 1 tsp vanilla extract
11. 1/2 tsp rum extract
12. 1/2 cup eggnog
13. Frosting
14. 1/2 cup butter, at room temperature (I used 1/4 cup salted and 1/4 cup unsalted butter)
15. 3 - 5 Tbsp eggnog
16. 1/2 tsp rum extract
17. 3 cups powdered sugar

DIRECTIONS:
Preheat oven to 350 degrees. In a mixing bowl, whisk together flour, baking powder, salt, nutmeg and cinnamon for 30 seconds, set aside. In the bowl of an electric stand mixer fitted with the paddle attachment, whip together butter, granulated sugar and brown sugar until pale and fluffy. Mix in egg yolks one at a time, blending just until combined after each addition. Mix in vanilla extract, rum extract and egg nog.

With mixer set on low speed, slowly add in dry ingredients and mix just until combined. Scoop dough out by the heaping tablespoonfuls and drop onto Silpat or parchment paper lined baking sheets, spacing cookies 2-inches apart. Bake in preheated oven 11 - 13 minutes. Allow to rest on baking sheet several minutes before transferring to a wire rack to cool. Cool completely then frost with Eggnog Frosting and sprinkle tops lightly with nutmeg.

For the Eggnog Frosting:

In the bowl of an electric stand mixer fitted with the paddle attachment, whip butter until very pale and fluffy. Add in rum extract and 3 Tbsp eggnog and mix in powdered sugar. Add additional eggnog to reach desired consistency.

Lemon Love Cookies

INGREDINENTS:

1 cup butter, softened

1 cup powdered sugar

1 cup granulated sugar

2 large eggs

1 cup vegetable oil

1/4 cup fresh lemon juice

5 1/4 cups all-purpose flour

1 teaspoon cream of tartar

1 teaspoon baking soda

1/4 teaspoon salt

1 teaspoon grated lemon rind

3/4 cup plus 2 tablespoons raspberry jam

DIRECTIONS:

Beat butter at medium speed with an electric mixer until fluffy; add powdered and granulated sugars, beating well. Add eggs, oil, and lemon juice, beating until blended.

Combine flour and next 4 ingredients; gradually add to sugar mixture, beating until blended.

Shape dough into 1-inch balls, and place about 2 inches apart on lightly greased baking sheets. Press thumb in center of each cookie to make an indentation.

Bake, in batches, at 350° for 9 to 11 minutes or until set. (Do not brown.) Remove to wire racks to cool. Spoon 1/2 teaspoon raspberry jam in each indentation.

Mesmirizing Meringue Cookies

INGREDIENTS:
- 3egg whites
- 1 cup sugar
- 1/4 teaspoon salt
- 1 teaspoon vanila

DIRECTIONS:

1. Heat oven to 300 degrees.
2. Blend egg whites, sugar, salt and vanilla in top of double boiler.
3. Place over boiling water; beat with rotary beater, scraping bottom and side of pan occasionally, until mixture forms stiff peaks.
4. Drop mixture by teaspoonfuls onto 2 lightly greased baking sheets.
5. (Drop all mixture onto the 2 baking sheets; bake only 1 baking sheet at a time.) Bake 12 to 15 minutes or until light brown.
6. Immediately remove from baking sheet.

Delicious Dark Chocolate Walnut Cookies

INGREDIENTS:

1 1/3 cups unbleached all-purpose flour

2/3 cup unsweetened cocoa powder

3/4 teaspoon baking soda

1/2 teaspoon salt

12 tablespoons (1 1/2 sticks) unsalted butter, softened to room temperature

1 1/4 cups cups packed light brown sugar

1/2 teaspoon vanilla extract

2 large eggs

4 ounces good-quality bittersweet or semi-sweet chocolate morsels or chopped chocolate pieces

3/4 cup coarsely chopped walnuts

Flaky sea salt

DIRECTIONS:

Preheat oven to 375°F with a rack in the center of the oven. Line a cookie sheets with a piece of parchment, or a baking mat.

Sift the flour, cocoa powder, baking soda, and salt into a mixing bowl.

In a stand mixer or with a hand-held electric mixer on medium speed (or by hand) beat together the butter, brown sugar, and vanilla until fluffy and uniform in color. Add the eggs one at a time, beating until combined. Reduce the speed to low and add the dry mixture, mixing until just combined. Add the chocolate and walnut pieces, and stir to combine.

Drop heaping tablespoons of dough on the baking sheet, leaving at least 2 inches of space in between. Sprinkle a small pinch of salt on top of each cookie.

Bake until puffed, but still soft and slightly shiny in the middle, about 12 minutes. Transfer the cookies to a cooling rack. Serve warm, or store at room temperature for up to 3 days in an airtight container.

Stained Glass Windows Cookies

INGREDIENTS:

For the biscuits
- 350g/12oz plain flour, plus extra for dusting
- 1 tsp bicarbonate of soda
- ½ tsp salt
- 2 tsp ground ginger
- 100g/3½oz butter
- 175g/6oz soft brown sugar
- 1 free-range egg, beaten
- 4 tbsp golden syrup
- packet wrapped fruit-flavoured boiled sweets in different colours

To decorate
- tube ready-made white icing (available in the baking sections of most supermarkets) (optional)
- narrow ribbon

DIRECTIONS:
1. Preheat the oven to 180C/350F/Gas 4.
2. For the biscuits, mix the flour, bicarbonate of soda, salt and ginger together in a bowl.
3. Rub in the butter until the mixture resembles fine breadcrumbs, then stir in the sugar.In another bowl, beat together the egg and golden syrup, then pour this mixture into the flour mixture and mix to make a smooth dough, kneading lightly with your hands.h
4. Crush the sweets in their wrappers using a rolling pin.
5. Roll the dough out on a floured work surface to about 0.5cm/¼in thick, then cut into shapes using a selection of

Christmas-themed cookie cutters. Transfer the biscuits to baking sheets lined with baking paper.

6. Cut out shapes in the centre of each biscuit, making sure you leave a good edge all around the biscuit. Completely fill the hole in each biscuit with crushed boiled sweets.

7. Make a hole at the top of each biscuit using a drinking straw so that you will be able to thread a ribbon through it later. Bake the biscuits in the oven for 10-12 minutes, or until golden-brown.

8. Remove the biscuits from the oven. While they're still warm, check that the holes are still there - if not, push a straw through again. Do not remove the biscuits from the baking tray until they have cooled because the boiled sweets need to harden. Once the sweets have hardened, gently lift the biscuits onto a wire rack with a palette knife to finish cooling.

9. If you like, you can decorate the biscuits with piped white icing. Thread ribbons through the holes in the biscuits to make loops for hanging from the tree.

Raspberry Swirl Surprise Cookies

INGREDIENTS:
- 2 cups all purpose flour
- 1 teaspoon baking powder
- 1/4 teaspoon salt
- 1/2 cup (1 stick) unsalted butter, room temperature
- 1 cup sugar
- 1 large egg
- 1 teaspoon vanilla extract
- 1/2 cup raspberry jam
- 1/2 cup sweetened flaked coconut
- 1/4 cup chopped toasted walnuts

DIRECTIONS:

1. Start by sifting the flour, baking powder, and salt into medium bowl. Using an electric mixer, beat butter in large bowl until smooth. Add sugar and beat until blended. Beat in egg and vanilla. Add flour mixture and beat until moist clumps form. Gather dough into ball. Flatten and shape into rectangle. Wrap in plastic and refrigerate until cold, at least 1 hour. (Can be made 1 day ahead. Keep refrigerated.

2. Soften dough slightly before rolling out.)

3. Roll out dough on lightly floured surface to 13x10-inch rectangle (about 1/4 inch thick). Mix jam and coconut in small bowl to blend. Spread over dough, leaving 1/2-inch plain border.

Sprinkle nuts evenly over jam mixture. Starting at one long side, roll up dough jellyroll style into 13x2 1/2-inch log. Wrap in plastic and chill 30 minutes.

4.Preheat oven to 375°F. Line 2 baking sheets with parchment paper. Unwrap cookie log; cut 1/2 inch off each end and discard. Cut remaining log crosswise into 1/2-inch-thick rounds. Arrange rounds, cut side down, on prepared sheets, spacing 1 inch apart; reshape into neat rounds, if desired. Bake cookies until edges and bottom are golden, about 20 minutes. Transfer cookies to racks and cool.

Great Griscotti

INGREDIENTS:

3 cups all-purpose flour

1 1/2 cups instant grits

1 tablespoon baking powder

1 teaspoon kosher salt

1 1/2 cups sugar

3/4 cup butter, softened

1 tablespoon loosely packed orange zest

4 large eggs

1 1/2 cups sweetened dried cranberries

PARCHMENT PAPER

DIRECTIONS:

1. Preheat oven to 325°. Stir together first 4 ingredients. Beat sugar, butter, and zest at medium speed with an electric mixer until creamy. Add eggs, 1 at a time, beating well after each addition. Add flour mixture and cranberries, beating just until blended.

2. Divide dough into 3 equal portions; shape each into a 12 1/2- x 9-inch slightly flattened log, using lightly floured hands. Place about 2 inches apart on a parchment paper-lined baking sheet. Bake at 325° for 30 to 35 minutes or until light brown. Transfer to wire racks; cool 15 minutes. Reduce oven temperature to 300°.

3. Cut each log into 1/4- to 1/2-inch-thick slices using a serrated knife. Place on 3 parchment paper-lined baking sheets.

4. Bake at 300° for 30 to 35 minutes or until golden brown. Cool on baking sheets 10 minutes; transfer cookies, on parchment paper, to wire racks, and cool.

Easy Peezy Pumpkin Cookies

INGREDIENTS:

- 1 (14 ounce) can 100% pure pumpkin
- 2 eggs
- 1/2 cup applesauce
- 1/2 teaspoon vanilla extract
- 1 (18.25 ounce) package spice cake mix
- 1 teaspoon cinnamon
- 1/2 teaspoon ground nutmeg
- 1/4 teaspoon ground cloves

DIRECTIONS:
Preheat oven to 350 degrees F (175 degrees C). Lightly grease two baking sheets.
Beat the pumpkin, eggs, applesauce, and vanilla together in a large mixing bowl. Stir in the cake mix, cinnamon, nutmeg, and cloves until well blended and creamy.
Drop by spoonfulls on baking sheets
Bake in preheated oven for 8-10 minutes

Happy Honey Hazelnut Cookies

INGREDIENTS:
3/4 cup powdered sugar

1/2 cup butter, softened

1 tablespoon honey

1/4 teaspoon vanilla extract

1/8 teaspoon kosher salt

1/2 cup finely chopped hazelnuts

6 tablespoons all-purpose flour

3 tablespoons whole wheat flour

PARCHMENT PAPER

DIRECTIONS:
1. Preheat oven to 325°. Beat first 5 ingredients at medium speed with an electric mixer 4 to 5 minutes or until creamy. Add hazelnuts and next 2 ingredients; beat just until blended. Drop by level teaspoonfuls 3 inches apart onto 2 parchment paper-lined baking sheets.
2. Bake at 325° for 12 to 14 minutes or until edges are golden brown. Cool on baking sheets 5 minutes; transfer to wire racks, and cool.
Hazelnut Fig Sandwiches: Prepare as directed. Spoon 1/2 cup fig preserves on half of cookies (about 1 tsp. per cookie); top with remaining cookies. Makes about 2 dozen.

Delicious Paleo Christmas Recipes

Drinks

Yule-Time Pumpkin Latte

Prep Time: 10 minutes
Servings: 1
    Ingredients:
1 cup coconut milk
1/4 cup pumpkin puree
1/4 teaspoon of each—cloves, cinnamon, allspice, nutmeg
Directions:
1. In a sauce pan, heat milk over medium heat.
2. Add puree and spices.
3. Stir until completely dissolved.

Santa's Sangria

Prep Time: 10 minutes
Servings: 15-20
   Ingredients:
1 bottle of red win
1 cup brandy
1 cup triple sec
1 cup syrup
1 cup lemonade
1 apple, diced
1 can club soda

Directions:
1. In a sauce pan, mix syrup and sugar and stir until completely dissolved.
2. In punch bowl, mix wine, brandy and triple sec with syrup mixture. Mix well before adding lemonade and diced apples.
3. Pour club soda and serve over ice.

Paleo Eggnog

Prep Time: 15 minutes
Servings: 2-3

Ingredients:

6 plump dates
1 tablespoon raw cashews
1 cup unsweetened almond milk
1/2 cup coconut milk
1/2 teaspoon pure vanilla extract
1/2 teaspoon cinnamon
1/4 teaspoon nutmeg

Directions:

1. Combine dates and cashews in a bowl and pour hot water over it. Let it soak to soften.
2. Once ready, place inside a food processor until fine and smooth, along with water and the rest of the ingredients and process until smooth.
3. Pour into two glasses and serve.

Creamy Christmas Cider

Prep Time: 15 minutes
Servings: 4

Ingredients:

1 cup pumpkin puree
1 cup pure apple juice
1 cup coconut milk
1 teaspoon ground cinnamon
1/4 teaspoon ground nutmeg

Directions:

1. Combine pumpkin, juice and milk in a saucepan over medium heat.
2. Allow mixture to simmer while constantly stirring.
3. Add cinnamon and nutmeg and remove from heat.
4. Strain to remove solids before serving.

Cranberry Christmas Cocktail

Prep Time: 15 minutes
Servings: 2
Ingredients:
3 large pink grapefruits, chilled
5 Valencia oranges, juiced
2 lbs fresh cranberries, washed and drained
4 tablespoon raw honey
4 jiggers Chopin potato vodka
2 star anise
2 eyedroppers liquid stevia
1/2 teaspoon. orange oil
1/4 teaspoon of sea salt
Directions:
1. Combine the juices of all fruits over a saucepan.
2. Add anise and let mixture simmer.
3. Strain and place back in a saucepan with cranberries. Let it simmer for 40-45 minutes until it all bursts.
4. Remove from heat and add honey, orange oil and liquid stevia.
5. Pour mixture in cocktail shakers and pour over ice.

Starters

Paleo Holiday Starters

Prep Time: 30 minutes
Servings: 10-15
 Ingredients:
1 large watermelon, seeded and cubed
1 pack small cherries, stems removed
2 bunch of green grapes
2 honeydew melons, cubed
Directions:
1. Skewer fruits in long toothpicks alternating between red and green fruits.
2. Serve chilled.

Beef And Bacon Balls

Prep Time: 30 minutes
Servings: 12
  Ingredients:
1.5lbs ground beef
6 slices of bacon, cut into 1 inch pieces
1/2 yellow onion, diced
1 egg, whisked
1/4 cup almond flour
1 teaspoon cumin
1/2 teaspoon chili powder
salt and pepper, to taste
Directions:
1. Set oven to 350 degrees.
2. Saute bacon over medium heat and add onions until tender.
3. Add ground beef, egg, almond flour and seasonings.
4. Remove from heat and allow mixture to cool.
5. Take a heaping tablespoon and roll into balls.
6. Arrange on a baking sheet and bake for 10-15 minutes.

Paleo Pinwheel Bites

Prep Time: 30 minutes
Servings: 10-12
Ingredients:
2 zucchini
1 bunch fresh basil
2 packs of Applegate prosciutto
1 lemon
Directions:
1. Slice zucchini lengthwise.
2. Place prosciutto on a plate and layer a zucchini along the length of the vegetable. Top with basil leaves and roll. Secure with a toothpick.
3. Repeat until you have gone through all the ingredients.
4. Squeeze lemon over it and chill in the refrigerator before serving.

Egg Cups

Prep Time: 30 minutes
Servings: 10
Ingredients:
1 tablespoon olive oil
1 red onion, diced
1 tablespoon tomato paste
2 cups tomatoes, diced
1 cup pepperoni, diced
10 eggs, beaten
1 teaspoon salt
1 teaspoon dried oregano
1 teaspoon black pepper
1 cup black olives

Directions:
1. Saute onions in olive oil until tender.
2. Add tomato paste and tomatoes followed by pepperoni.
3. In a sepate bowl, add eggs and herbs. Season well.
4. Pour mixture into muffin tins and divide tomato mixture into the egg muffins.
5. Bake at 325 degrees for 25-30 minutes.

Garlic And Almond Thins

Prep Time: 20 minutes
Servings: 8
Ingredients:
1 cup almond flour
1 egg white
1 pinch sea salt
1 teaspoon garlic powder
Directions:
1. Set oven to 325 degrees.
2. Combine almond flour, egg white and salt and mix until you form a paste.
3. Line a baking sheet with parchment paper and flatten batter onto it.
4. Cover with another piece of parchment paper and bake at 325 degrees for 10 minutes until very lightly browned.
5. Break apart once cooked and serve.

Macadamia And Cashew Cream And Crackers

Prep Time: 2 hours
Servings: 6-8
 Ingredients:
1/3 cup hemp hearts
1/3 cup pine nuts
1/3 cup nut of macadamia and cashew
1/2 cup almond milk
1 tablespoon greek spice mix
1 loaf French bread, sliced
Directions:

1. Combine all ingredients in a food processor, except milk, until it turns into a smooth paste.
2. Gradually add milk until mixture is smooth and creamy.
3. Serve with sliced French bread.

Holiday Spiced Nuts

Prep Time: 20 minutes
Servings: 12-15
    Ingredients:
2 tablespoons ghee, melted
1 1/2 teaspoons ground cumin
1/2 teaspoon paprika
1/4 teaspoon cinnamon
2 1/2 cup assorted nut--almonds, pecans, cashews, and macadamias
2 tablespoons brown sugar
1 teaspoon salt

Directions:
1. Set oven to 300 degrees.
2. Over medium heat, mix cumin, cayenne and paprika with ghee until fragrant.
3. Place nuts in a bowl and pour ghee mixture over it with sugar and salt.
4. Mix to make sure it's all coated.

Bacon And Sweet Potato Casserole

Prep Time: 40 minutes
Servings: 8

Ingredients:
1 tablespoon coconut oil
1 medium sweet potato, peeled and sliced into 1/8" thin rounds
1/4 teaspoon salt
8 eggs
1/2 teaspoon herbs de provence
1/2 cup carrots, peeled and shredded
1/2 cup zucchini, peeled and shredded
3/4 lbs sliced sugar-free nitrate-free beef bacon

Directions:
1. Line bottom of a baking dish with sweet potatoes.
2. Whisk eggs with seasoning and add carrots and zucchini.
3. Pour mixture over sweet potatoes.
4. Top with bacon strips.
5. Bake for 30 minutes at 400 degrees.

Salads And Side Dishes

Asparagus Wrapped In Proscuitto

Prep Time: 25 minutes
Servings: 8-10
Ingredients:
18 asparagus spears
9-10 slices of prosciutto
Some ghee for frying
Directions:
1. Wrap a strip of prosciutto around an asparagus.
2. Repeat until you have gone through all the ingredients.
3. Fry assembled asparagus spears in ghee until asparagus is tender and prosciutto is almost crisp.

Holiday Paleo Buns

Prep Time: 30 minutes
Servings: 6-8
Ingredients:
1 box Chebe original bread mix (grain-free, made with cassava flour)
2 tablespoon organic palm shortening
2 large eggs
1/4 cup water
Directions:
1. Set oven to 375 degrees.
2. Combine bread mix with 2 tablespoon of oil, eggs and add water.
3. Knead until smooth and divide into rolls.
4. Bake for 18-20 minutes until lightly browned.

Green Casserole

Prep Time: 20 minutes
Servings: 4
   Ingredients:
1 lb kale, cleaned and torn into bite size pieces
2 tablespoon ghee
8 oz mushrooms, roughly chopped
4 cloves garlic, minced
1/2 yellow onion, diced
1 cup almond cream
1/2 yellow onion, finely sliced
1/4 c fat of choice
Salt and pepper, to taste
Directions:
1. Set oven to 350 degrees.
2. Saute mushrooms, garlic and onions in ghee.
3. Boil water in a separate sauce pan and add kale. Once cooked, dunk kale in ice water. Squeeze liquids from the leaves and place in a deep casserole dish.
4. Take mushroom mixture and blend until fine in a food processor.
5. Place back in the sauté pan and add cream. Pour mixture into the casserole dish and mix well.
6. Place dish in the oven until mixture is bubbly.

Christmas Fauxtatoes

Prep Time: 90 minutes
Servings: 4-6
    Ingredients:
1 head cauliflower, stemmed and roughly chopped
1 bulb fennel, roughly chopped
3 cloves garlic
fat of choice
1 cup chicken or veggie stock
salt & pepper
Method
Directions:
1. Set oven to 400 degrees.
2. Roast cauliflower and fennel with salt and pepper for about 30 minutes.
3. Place cauliflower, fennel and garlic in a food processor.
4. Slow add stock until you achieve desired consistency.

Red And Green Paleo Salad

Prep Time: 30 minutes
Servings: 6-8

Ingredients:

2 cups fresh cranberries
4-5 cloves of garlic unpeeled
1/3 cup olive oil
1/4 cup fresh lemon juice
1 Tbs Dijon mustard
2rsp fresh lemon peel
1 bunch kale chopped w/o stems
1 am bulb fennel cored & shaved or cut in very thin wedges
1 cup chopped walnuts toasted
1/2 cup thinly sliced red pepper & red onion

Directions:

1. Set oven to 375 degrees.
2. Line baking sheet with foil and add cranberries and garlic.
3. Sprinkle with oil and salt and pepper.
4. Roast for 30 minutes until tender and browned.
5. To mix dressing—mix oil, lemon juice, mustard and lemon peel in a mason jar and shake vigorously. Strain.
6. Mix cranberries, fennel, kale and peppers with onion in a bowl and toss with prepared dressing.
7. Sprinkle with nuts.

Entrees

Herb Crusted Roasted Lamb

Prep Time: 30 minutes
Servings: 3
   Ingredients:
4 lamb chops
1 and a bit cup macadamia nuts, finely chopped
1 large garlic clove, peeled
1/2 cup chopped parsley
4 tbsp olive oil
2/3 tsp Celtic salt
A little extra salt and black pepper
Some ghee for cooking
2 tablespoons assorted herbs—rosemary, dill, paprika

Directions:
1. Combine garlic, olive oil with parsley, herbs and salt and pepper as well as macadamia nuts.
2. Take a lamb chop and dredge into the herb mixture. Repeat for all pieces.
3. In a skillet, sear lamb chops in ghee and season with some sea salt.

Savory Cinnamon Pork

Prep Time: 60 minutes
Servings: 6-8
      Ingredients:
3 tablespoons olive oil
3 garlic cloves, minced
1 tablespoon chili powder
1/2 tablespoon ground cinnamon
1 pork tenderloin
Salt and pepper to taste
Directions:
1. Set oven to 400 degrees.
2. Mix chili powder with cinnamon and olive oil. Rub mixture onto pork.
3. Marinate for half an hour.
4. Once ready, heat a grill pan and cook pork until browned—aroudn 3 minutes per side.
5. Place in a baking dish and bake for 15-20 mintues.

Salmon In Saffron

Prep Time: 30 minutes
Servings: 2-4
      Ingredients:
1.8 lb Salmon in cubes, skinned and deboned
1 Large Leek washed and chopped
2 Granny Smith apple chopped
3 cups water
15 gram/230 grain chicken broth
1/2 gram/8 grain Saffron
1 tsp Fresh Thyme
sea salt and pepper to taste
Directions:
1. Boil water with chicken broth, thyme, saffron, salt and pepper.
2. Add apple and leek and allow to boil.
3. Drain and place back in a sauté pan and add salmon. Cook for 5 minutes.

Herb Roasted Turkey Breast

Prep Time: 8-10 hours
Servings: 6-8
    Ingredients:
4-6lb Turkey Breasts with Skin On
2 sprigs Fresh Rosemary
1 cup Fresh Basil
1/2 cup Fresh Taragon
1 tablespoon sea salt
1 tablespoon Black Pepper
4-5 Slices of Cooked Bacon
2-3 Tbsp Olive Oil
Directions:
1. Set oven to 325 degrees.
2. Apply oil onto turkey breasts.
3. Pulse herbs and seasonings with bacon in a food processor.
4. Rub mixture onto turkey breasts inside and over the skin.
5. Arrange on a baking sheet and bake for an hour.
6. Turn the pieces and drizzle drippings over it and cook for an additional hour.

Bacon And Wild Mushroom Steaks

Prep Time: 20 minutes
Servings: 2-3

Ingredients:

2 cups cremini mushrooms, sliced
1 cup chanterelle mushrooms, torn into pieces
10 strips bacon, sliced crosswise in 1/2 inch pieces
1/2 white onion, sliced
2 cloves garlic, minced
1/4 teaspoon fresh thyme, finely chopped
1/2 cup low sodium beef stock (or chicken stock)
2 tablespoon balsamic vinegar
Salt and pepper to taste
2 rib eye steaks, grilled, broiled or pan fried
kale, steamed
cherry tomatoes, roasted

Directions:
1. Fry bacon until crisp and set aside.
2. Use bacon fat to sauté onions until tender. Add mushrooms, garlic and thyme.
3. Add stock and balsamic vinegar, bacon and season with salt and pepper.
4. In a separate skillet, over high heat, sear steaks.
5. Place kale and tomatoes on a plate, top with steak and mushroom mixture.
6. Repeat until you have assembled all ingredients together.

Stuffed Pork Chops

Prep Time: 90 minutes
Servings: 6

Ingredients:

6 1" thick pocket pork chops
2 tablespoon olive oil
2 medium baking apples (Gala and York are our favorites), peeled, cored and diced
10 strips of bacon, diced
1 red onion, diced
2 cloves garlic, minces
4 fresh sage leaves, finely chopped
1/4 teaspoon paprika
1 tablespoon lemon juice
1 tablespoon salt
1/2 teaspoon pepper

Directions:
1. Saute apples, bacon and onion in olive oil until tender.
2. Add garlic, paprika and sage and drizzle with lemon juice.
3. Mix well and remove from heat.
4. Stuff mixture into the pork chop pockets.
5. Sear chops over high heat for 5 minutes on each side.
6. Place pork chops on a baking dish at 350 degrees for 30-35 minutes.

Stuffed Squash

Prep Time: 60 mintues
Servings: 3-6
      Ingredients:
3 Acorn Squashes
1 lb Ground Meat
1 Onion, diced
2 Granny Smith Apples, chopped
1 cup Pecans, chopped
1 cup Fresh Cranberries
3 Large Carrots, grated
Olive Oil
1 cup Dry Red Wine
2 Eggs
Directions:

1. Brown meat in oil and add apples, onions, pecans, carrots, cranberries, wine, salt and pepper.
2. Slice acorn squashes in half and remove seeds. Place in a baking dish, facing down and add about 2 cups of water. Bake for 30 minutes at 350 degrees.
3. Beat eggs and add to the ground beef mixture.
4. Once squash is ready, remove and divide filling between each.
5. Place back in the oven and bake for 40 minutes.

Desserts

Choco Almond Bites

Prep Time: 2 hours
Servings: 8-12
Ingredients:
1 cup Pure Almond Butter
1 cup Unsweetened Chocolate
1/2 cup Coconut Sugar
2 tablespoons Grapeseed Oil
1 cup almonds, chopped
Directions:
1. Melt chocolate using a double boiler add add oil and coconut sugar. Stir until smooth.
2. Take a teaspoon and roll into balls and roll over chopped almonds.
3. Place on a baking sheet and refrigerate until it sets.

Mint Chocolate Squares

Prep Time: Overnight
Servings: 15
Ingredients:
1 cup almonds
1 cup walnuts
10 large medjool dates, pitted
2 pinches salt
1/4 – 1/2 tsp peppermint extract
1 1/2 tsp vanilla
1 tsp cinnamon
1/2 cup shredded coconut
3 Tbsp cacao powder
1/2 – 1 Tbsp honey

Directions:
1. Place nuts in a food processor with dates and blend until you achieve a sticky paste.
2. Add all remaining ingredients and blend.
3. Adjust sweetness and peppermint according to taste.
4. Pour batter into a baking pan and top with cinnamon and shredded coconut.
5. Place in a refrigerator overnight to set.

Macadamia Apple Crispies

Prep Time: 2 hours
Servings: 6-8
      Ingredients:
Filling
5-6 apples peeled and coarsely chopped
4 tablespoons butter, diced
1 tablespoon lemon juice
1 teaspoon ground cinnamon
Topping
1 cup blanched almond flour
3/4 cup macadamia nuts, coarsely chopped
3/4 cup pecans and/or walnuts, coarsely chopped
2 tablespoons palm sugar
1 tablespoon cinnamon
1/2 teaspoon ginger
Pinch of nutmeg
4 tablespoons coconut oil

Directions:
1. Set oven to 350 degrees.
2. Mix apples, lemon juiced, butter and cinnamon in a pie dish and bake until tender.
3. Combine dry ingredients in a separate bowl. Add coconut oil until you achive a crumbly and moist mixture.
4. Remove apple mixture from the oven and mix crumble topping over apples.
5. Place back in the oven for another 10 mintues.

Chocolate Cream Cups

Prep Time: 2 hours
Servings: 8
    Ingredients:
1 cup shredded unsweetened coconut
1 canfull fat unsweetened coconut milk
1/2 cup coconut butter
1/2 cup coco powder
1/4 cup blue agave nectar
1 teaspoon vanilla
1/2 teaspoon sea salt
Crust
1 cup whole raw almonds
1/2 cup dates, finely chopped
2 tablespoon coconut oil
Directions:
1. Beat coconut milk, coconut butter, agave nectar and vanilla with a mixer until smooth.
2. Add coconut coco powder and mix thoroughly. Place in a refrigerator to chill.
3. Set oven to 300 degrees.
4. To make the crust--process almonds and dates until you achieve a fine paste. Add 2 tablespoons of coconut oil. Divide and press mixture onto cupcake molds.
5. Scoop a tablespoon of the coconut mixture into the crust and chill for at least 2 hours.

Slow Cooked Apple Pecan Crisp

Prep Time: 2 hours
Servings: 8-12
    Ingredients:
6 medium-size crisp tart apples
1 teaspoon ground cinnamon
1/2 cup shredded coconut
1/3 cup packed palm sugar
1/4 cup almond flour
1/2 cup cold grass-fed butter, cut into small pieces
1/2 cup chopped pecans
1/2 cup of raw honey

Directions:
1. Combine apples and cinnamon and place in a slow cooker.
2. Whisk coconut, glour, butter and sugar until mixture is crumbly.
3. Sprinkle crumbs over apples and stir in pecans and honey.
4. Cook on low for 4-6 hours.

Christmas Casserole Recipes

Christmas Morning Casserole

Prep Time: Overnight
Servings: 4-6
  Ingredients:
1 pound ground pork sausage
1 teaspoon mustard powder
1/2 teaspoon salt
4 eggs, beaten
2 cups milk
6 slices white bread, toasted and cut into cubes
8 ounces mild Cheddar cheese, shredded
Directions:
1. Crumble sausage and sauté until browned.
2. Whisk salt, mustard powder, eggs and milk.
3. Add sausage into the mixture, bread cubes and cheese.
4. Pour mixture into a casserole dish and refrigerate overnight.
5. Bake for 45 to 60 minutes at 350 degrees, covered.
6. Remove cover and bake for an additional half an hour.

Herbed Bacon And Mushroom Casserole

Prep Time: 90 minutes
Servings: 6-9
      Ingredients:
1 pound bacon
2 onions, chopped
2 cups fresh sliced mushrooms
1 tablespoon butter
4 cups frozen hash brown potatoes, thawed
1 teaspoon salt
1/4 teaspoon garlic salt
1/2 teaspoon ground black pepper
4 eggs
1 1/2 cups milk
1 pinch dried parsley
1 cup shredded Cheddar cheese

Directions:
1. Fry bacon until crisp and crumble.
2. Using the same skillet, cook mushrooms and onions until tender.
3. Grease a casserole dish with butter and place hash brown at the bottom. Season with salt, pepper and garlic salt.
4. Top with bacon and mushroom mixture.
5. Whisk eggs, milk and parsley together and pour mixture into the casserole.
6. Top with shredded cheese.
7. Bake for an hour at 400 degrees.

Baked Christmas Brunch Casserole

Prep Time: Overnight
Servings: 6-8
    Ingredients:
6 eggs
1/2 teaspoon black pepper
1/2 teaspoon Worcestershire sauce
Dash of pepper sauce
3 cups milk
2 tablespoons butter or margarine, melted
1 loaf sliced white bread
1/4 cup finely chopped onion
1/4 cup finely chopped green pepper
1/2 teaspoon dry mustard
1/2 pound thinly sliced or shaved ham
2 cups shredded Cheddar cheese

Directions:
1. Remove crusts from bread and place bread at the bottom of a baking dish.
2. Layer with ham and sprinkle with cheese. Put on with another layer of bread.
3. Whisk eggs, green pepper, dry mustard and onions. Season with pepper and add Worcestershire sauce and Tabasco. Mix thoroughly.
4. Pour over bread and cover. Refrigerate overnight.
5. Bake in the oven for 1 to 1 1/2 hours.

Red And Green Holiday Casserole

Prep Time: 60 minutes
Servings: 6-10
　　　Ingredients:
1 pack cottage cheese
2 cups diced tomatoes
6 eggs
1/2 cup all-purpose flour
1/4 cup sour cream
2 teaspoons salt
1/2 teaspoon ground black pepper
2 packs frozen chopped spinach, thawed and drained
4 cups shredded Cheddar cheese, divided

Directions:
1. Set oven to 350 degrees.
2. Combine cottage cheese, flour, salt and pepper with eggs and sour cream in a food processor.
3. Place spinach, cottage cheese mixture and 2 cups of cheddar in a bowl. Mix well and add tomatoes; pour into a casserole dish.
4. Bake for 45 minutes.
5. Remove and top with remaining cheese and bake until cheese has melted.

Creamy Artichoke Casserole

Prep Time: 60 mintues
Servings: 6-8
    Ingredients:
1 cup sour cream
1 can water chestnuts, drained and chopped
3/4 cup grated Parmesan cheese
3/4 cup real mayonnaise
2 teaspoons garlic salt
1 tablespoon lemon juice
1 cup French fried onion rings
6 cloves garlic, roasted and unpeeled
4 packs frozen chopped spinach - thawed, drained and squeezed dry
1 can artichoke hearts, drained and chopped
1/4 cup butter
1 pack sliced fresh mushrooms
3 green onions, finely chopped
1 pack cream cheese, softened

Directions:
1. Set oven to 350 degrees.
2. Combine spinach and artichoke hearts in a bowl.
3. Saute mushrooms in butter and add green onions. Pour mixture into the spinach and mi well.
4. Stir in soft cream cheese into the spinach mixture.
5. Add sour cream, water chestnuts, parmesan cheese, garlic salt, mayonnaise and lemon juice.
6. Remove skins from roasted garlic and mix in with the spinach.
7. Transfer mixture to a casserole dish and bake for 30 minutes until mixture is bubbly.

Buttered Salmon And Croissant Casserole

Prep Time: 70 minutes
Servings: 6

Ingredients:

6 croissants, split - tops set aside and bottoms torn into 1-inch pieces
2 green onions, thinly sliced
4 ounces smoked salmon, chopped
1 cup shredded Monterey Jack cheese
1 cup shredded Swiss cheese
1 cup shredded mozzarella cheese
2 tablespoons chopped fresh dill
1 teaspoon salt
freshly cracked black pepper to taste
3 tablespoons butter
1/2 white onion, chopped
2 cloves garlic, minced
12 eggs
1/2 cup milk

Directions:
1. Set oven to 400 degrees.
2. Saute onion and garlic in butter until tender.
3. Whisk eggs and milk together.
4. Place croissant bottoms at the bottom of a casserole dish.
5. Add onions and garlic; green onions, smoked salmon and shredded cheese. Sprinkle with chopped dill.
6. Pour egg mixture over it and top with a sprinkle with salt and pepper.
7. Place croissant tops over the casserole.
8. Bake for 50 minutes.

Make-Ahead Christmas Casserole

Prep Time: 7-8 hours
Servings: 12
    Ingredients:
3/4 cup shredded Swiss cheese
1/2 cup milk
1 tablespoon chopped fresh parsley
1 teaspoon garlic salt
1/4 teaspoon ground black pepper
4 thin slices tomato
1 1/2 teaspoons chopped fresh parsley
1 pack frozen hashbrown potatoes, thawed
1/3 cup vegetable oil
1 pack pork breakfast sausage
6 eggs, beaten
1 cup sliced fresh mushrooms
3/4 cup shredded pepperjack cheese
Directions:
1. Set oven to 425 degrees.
2. Toss hash browns in oil and press onto the bottom of a baking dish.
3. Bake for about 30 minutes and remove. Lower temperature to 350 degrees.
4. Crumble sausages and sauté until evenly browned.
5. Add eggs, mushrooms, cheeses, milk and parsley, garlic salt and pepper in a bowl and mix well.
6. Pour into a casserole dish and add sausages.
7. Place tomato slices over the casserole and bake for until eggs set.

Leftover Holiday Ham And Potato Casserole

Prep Time: 40 minutes
Servings: 6

Ingredients:

6 small potatoes, peeled and cubed
3 tablespoons butter
2 cups cubed fully cooked ham
1 small onion, finely chopped
1/4 cup butter
3 tablespoons all-purpose flour
1 1/2 cups milk
salt and ground black pepper to taste
1 (8 ounce) package shredded Cheddar cheese
1/4 cup bread crumbs

Directions:

1. Boil potatoes in water until tender—about 20 minutes.
2. Set oven to 350 degrees.
3. Saute ham and onions in butter and cook until fragrant.
4. Add potatoes in the mixture. Mix well and transfer to a baking dish.
5. Combine melted butter and flour and whisk until smooth.
6. Slow add milk into the mixture and season with salt and pepper. Cook until mixture thickens.
7. Lower heat and add cheese into the sauce, stir until smooth and pour into the baking dish.
8. Bake until mixture starts to bubble.

Savory French Toast Bakes

Prep Time: 40 minutes
Servings: 8

Ingredients:

6 slices whole wheat bread, or more to taste
1 tablespoon butter, or as needed
12 slices deli ham, or more to taste
6 slices Swiss cheese, or more to taste
1/2 cup milk
4 eggs
1 teaspoon Worcestershire sauce
1/2 teaspoon mustard powder
salt and ground black pepper to taste

Directions:

1. Set oven to 350 degrees.
2. Spread butter on each side of the bread slices and place at the bottom of a baking dish.
3. Top with ham slices and layer with cheese on top.
4. Whisk eggs, milk, Worcestershire sauce and mustard powder. Season with salt and pepper. Pour mixture into the baking dish and allow to soak for 15 minutes.
5. Bake for about 20 minutes.

Creamed Onion Casserole

Prep Time: 60 minutes
Servings: 6-8
Ingredients:
3/4 cup uncooked basmati rice
5 cups water, cooked
1/4 cup butter
3 pounds sweet onions, coarsely chopped
1 cup half-and-half cream
1 1/2 teaspoons salt
2 cups shredded Swiss cheese, divided

Directions:
1. Set oven to 350 degrees.
2. In a skillet, sauté onions in butter until tender.
3. Add half and half, salt and cheese. Add rice and mix through.
4. Transfer mixture into a casserole dish and bake uncovered for about an hour.

Garlic Cheddar Potato Casserole

Prep Time: 30 minutes
Servings: 6-8
    Ingredients:
5 large potatoes, peeled, cooked and sliced into chunks
1 cup sour cream
2 pack cream cheese
1 pinch garlic salt
2 cups shredded Cheddar cheese
Directions:
1. Set oven to 350 degrees.
2. Place cooked potatoes in a food processor and process with sour cream, cream cheese and garlic salt.
3. Place mixture in a casserole dish.
4. Sprinkle with cheddar cheese and bake for 20 minutes.

Creamy Baked Oyster Casserole

Prep Time: 60 minutes
Servings: 8
      Ingredients:
1 3/4 cups milk
1/2 cup butter
salt and pepper to taste
1 cup parmesan cheese
1 pint shucked oysters, cooked
8 oz saltine crackers, crushed
1 egg, beaten
Directions:
1. Set oven to 400 degrees.
2. Whisk eggs with 1/3 cup of milk.
3. Mix crushed crackers and oysters.
4. Place remaining crackers in a baking dish.
5. Pour milk mixture into the dish, just enough so it moistens the crackers.
6. Pour oysters into the dish and pour remaining milk mixture.
7. Sprinkle with salt and pepper and parmesan cheese.
8. Bake at 350 degrees for an hour.

Leftover Turkey And Potato Casserole

Prep Time: 8-10 hours
Servings: 8
     Ingredients:

1 can condensed cream of celery soup
3/4 cup milk
1 1/2 cups cooked turkey, cubed
1 package frozen green peas, thawed
3 cups stuffing
1 can French fried onions

Directions:
1. Set oven to 350 degrees.
2. Mix stuffing and 1/2 can of onions in a baking dish and press onto the sides and bottom of the baking dish.
3. Mix soup, milk, peas and leftover turkey into the shell.
4. Bake for half an hour for 30 minutes.
5. Remove from oven and top with remaining onions.
6. Bake for another 10 mintues.

Broccoli And Cheesy Rice Casserole

Prep Time: 20 minutes
Servings: 4-6
 Ingredients:
1/2 cup chopped celery
1 dash hot sauce
ground black pepper to taste
1 can French-fried onions
1 pack processed cheese, cubed
1 can condensed cream of chicken soup
1 cup cooked wild rice
1 pack frozen chopped broccoli, thawed
1/2 cup chopped onion

Directions:
1. Melt cheese in a microwave—about 1 to 2 minutes.
2. Add chicken soup, wild rice, onions, celery, broccoli, black pepper and hot sauce.
3. Microwave until mixture is bubbling.
4. Pour into a baking dish and sprinkle fried onions on top.
5. Cook in the oven for 10 minutes at 350 degrees.

Eggnog And Sweet Potato Casserole

Prep Time: 50 minutes
Servings: 6

Ingredients:

1/2 teaspoon salt
1/2 teaspoon ground ginger
1/4 teaspoon ground cloves
2 tablespoons grated orange zest
1/2 cup chopped pecans
2 cans sweet potatoes, mashed
1 cup eggnog
2 tablespoons butter, melted
3/4 cup white sugar

Directions:
1. Set an oven 375 degrees.
2. Combine eggnog, butter, salt, sugar, cloves, ginger, pecans and orange zest.
3. Pour mixture into a baking dish.
4. Bake in the oven for 40 minutes.

Creamed Corn Casserole

Prep Time: 4 hours
Servings: 8
Ingredients:
1 pack frozen corn, thawed
1 pint heavy whipping cream
2 cups Swiss cheese, shredded
2 eggs, lightly beaten
ground black pepper to taste
Directions:
1. Combine cream, cheese, corn and eggs in a bowl. Season with pepper.
2. Pour mixture in a slow cooker.
3. Cook for 4-5 hours on low.

Turkey And Mashed Potato Casserole

Prep Time: 60 minutes
Servings: 10-12
> **Ingredients**:

1 can condensed cream of mushroom soup
8 ounces cubed Cheddar cheese
8 ounces shredded Cheddar cheese
4 cups prepared mashed potatoes
1 pound turkey meat, cooked and shredded
1 onion, chopped
1 can green beans, drained

Directions:
1. Set oven to 350 degrees.
2. Arrange turkey at the bottom of a baking dish.
3. Top with onions and beans until turkey pieces are completely covered.
4. Pour soup over onions and beans.
5. Sprinkle with shredded cheese.
6. Combine cubed cheese and potatoes. Place over top of casserole and bake for 30-40 minutes.

Creamy Green Bean Casserole

Prep Time: 60 minutes
Servings: 6-8

Ingredients:

1/2 cup melted butter
1 can condensed cream of celery soup
1/2 cup sour cream
3/4 cup shredded Cheddar cheese
1/2 cup chopped onion
1 pinch salt
1 can French cut green beans, drained
1 can whole kernel corn, drained
2 sleeves buttery round crackers, crushed

Directions:

1. Set oven to 350 degrees.
2. Combine soup, cheddar, cream, onion and salt n a bowl.
3. Combine green beans and corn in a baking dish and pour soup mixture over it.
4. Mix crushed crackers and butter together and sprinkle over the casserole.
5. Bake for 45 minutes until topping is bubbly.

Baked Overnight Eggnog

Prep Time: 40 minutes
Servings: 4
      Ingredients:
1 cup brown sugar
1/2 cup butter
2 tablespoons light maple syrup
1 loaf French bread, cut into 1-inch slices
8 eggs
2 cups prepared eggnog
1/2 cup confectioner's sugar
Directions:

Combine brown sugar, butter, maple syrup in a sauce pan. Whisk until smooth.
Pour into a baking dish and place French bread on top.
Mix eggs and eggnog together and pour on top of the bread.
Cover and bake for 325 degrees for 20 minutes.
Remove and bake for an additional 5-7 minutes.
Sprinkle with confectioner's sugar before serving.

Creamy Layered Potatoes

Prep Time: 90 minutes
Servings: 6-8

Ingredients:

5 cloves garlic, minced
1 1/2 cups heavy cream
1 teaspoon salt
1/2 teaspoon black pepper
3 pounds red potatoes, peeled and sliced
3 tablespoons butter
6 ounces Gouda cheese, shredded, divided

Directions:

1. Set oven to 325 degrees.
2. In a baking dish, arrange potatoes so that it covers the bottom of the baking dish.
3. Place cheese on top to cover the potatoes.
4. Melt butter and sauté garlic until tender. Mix cream in and season with salt and pepper.
5. Pour over potatoes.
6. Bake for 75 minutes.

Part 2

Antipasto Cups

"Turn salami slices into appetizer shells to fill with the veggies and cheese of your choice. Melissa Obernesser, Utica, New York"

Serving: 2 dozen. | Ready in: 30 m

Ingredients:
- 24 slices Genoa salami (3-1/2 inches)
- 1 can (14 ounces) water-packed artichoke hearts
- 1 jar (8 ounces) marinated whole mushrooms
- 1 jar (8 ounces) roasted sweet red peppers
- 1/2 pound fresh mozzarella cheese, cut into 1/2-inch cubes
- 3 tablespoons olive oil
- 2 tablespoons red wine vinegar
- 1/2 teaspoon garlic salt
- 1/8 teaspoon pepper

Direction:

1. Preheat oven to 400degrees. Press half of the salami into 12 muffin cups. Loosely crumple aluminum foil to form twelve 2-in. balls; place in cups to keep salami from sliding. Bake until edges begin to brown, 6-8 minutes. Using tongs, remove from pans and invert onto paper towels to drain. Wipe muffin cups clean. Repeat with remaining salami, reusing foil balls., Meanwhile,

drain and coarsely chop artichoke hearts, mushrooms and red peppers; transfer to a small bowl. Stir in cheese. In another bowl, whisk oil, vinegar, garlic salt and pepper until blended. Drizzle over vegetable mixture; toss to coat. Using a slotted spoon, fill salami cups with vegetable mixture.

Nutrition Information:
- Calories: 87 calories
- Total Fat: 6g fat (3g saturated fat)
- Cholesterol: 16mg cholesterol
- Sodium: 325mg sodium
- Total Carbohydrate: 2g carbohydrate (1g sugars
- Protein: 5g protein.
- Fiber: 0 fiber) g

The Best Homemade Low Carb Keto Eggnog Velvety Smooth

"A special keto velvety & smooth drink to enjoy durning Winter Holidays"

Serving: 5 | Ready in: 30 m

Ingredients:
- 2 cups coconut milk / almond milk
- 1 cup heavy cream
- 4 large egg yolks
- 1/2 cup Swerve Sweetener (or Xylitol)
- 1 teaspoon freshly grated nutmeg
- 1 teaspoon cinnamon
- 1 teaspoon vanilla extract
- 1 cup dark rum/ whiskey

Direction:
1. In a bowl add the egg yolks and mix until they have a lighter colour.
2. Gradually add the sweetener and continue to whisk until completely dissolved.
3. In a medium saucepan, over high heat, combine the almond/ coconut milk, heavy cream, nutmeg, cinnamon.
4. Bring to a boil and stir occasionally.

5. Remove it from the heat, stir in the vanilla extract and the alcohol of your choice (dark rum).
6. Pour into a medium mixing bowl, and let it in the refrigerator to chill for at least an hour.

Nutrition Information:
- Calories: 326.09 kcal
- Total Fat: 22.44 g
- Saturated Fat: 12.71 g
- Sodium: 93.79 mg
- Total Carbohydrate: 3.24 g
- Protein: 3.75 g
- Fiber: 1.47 g
- Sugar: 1.62 g

Bacon Collard Greens

"A staple of Southern cuisine, these collard greens with bacon make for one incredible side dish. Marsha Ankeney, Niceville, Florida"

Serving: 9 servings. | Ready in: 01 h 20 m

Ingredients:
- 2 pounds collard greens
- 4 thick-sliced bacon strips, chopped
- 1 cup chopped sweet onion
- 5 cups reduced-sodium chicken broth
- 1 cup sun-dried tomatoes (not packed in oil), chopped
- 1/2 teaspoon garlic powder
- 1/4 teaspoon salt
- 1/4 teaspoon crushed red pepper flakes

Direction:
1. Trim thick stems from collard greens; coarsely chop leaves. In a Dutch oven, saute bacon for 3 minutes. Add onion; cook 8-9 minutes longer or until onion is tender and bacon is crisp. Add greens; cook just until wilted., Stir in remaining ingredients. Bring to a boil. Reduce heat; cover and simmer for 45-50 minutes or until greens are tender.

Nutrition Information:
- Calories: 157 calories

- Total Fat: 10g fat (4g saturated fat)
- Cholesterol: 12mg cholesterol
- Sodium: 651mg sodium
- Total Carbohydrate: 11g carbohydrate (4g sugars)
- Protein: 7g protein.
- Fiber: 5g fiber

Christmas Cauliflower Casserole

"This creamy casserole is filled with tender cauliflower and topped with a sprinkling of crispy herb stuffing. It's become a holiday classic that appeals to both kids and adults in our family. Carol Rex, Ocala, Florida"

Serving: 12 servings (3/4 cup each). | Ready in: 40 m

Ingredients:
- 3 packages (16 ounces each) frozen cauliflower
- 2 cups sour cream
- 2 cups shredded cheddar cheese
- 3 teaspoons chicken bouillon granules
- 1-1/2 teaspoons ground mustard
- 1/4 cup butter, cubed
- 1 cup stuffing mix
- 3/4 cup chopped walnuts

Direction:
1. Preheat oven to 375degrees. Cook cauliflower according to package directions; drain., In a large bowl, mix sour cream, cheese, bouillon and mustard until blended. Stir in cauliflower; transfer to a greased 13x9-in. baking dish., In a large skillet, heat butter over medium heat.

2. Add stuffing mix and walnuts; cook and stir until lightly toasted. Sprinkle over casserole. Bake, uncovered, 17-20 minutes or until heated
 hrough and topping is browned.

Nutrition Information:
- Calories: 276 calories
- Total Fat: 21g fat (11g saturated fat)
- Cholesterol: 57mg cholesterol
- Sodium: 476mg sodium
- Total Carbohydrate: 12g carbohydrate (4g sugars
- Protein: 10g protein.
- Fiber: 3g fiber)

Creamy Parmesan Spinach Bake

"This creamy, comforting side dish wonderfully rounds out any holiday dinner. Just a little of this rich casserole goes a long way. Jennifer Bley, Austin, Texas"

Serving: 12 servings (1/2 cup each). | Ready in: 55 m

Ingredients:
- 3 packages (9 ounces each) fresh baby spinach
- 1 small red onion, chopped
- 1 tablespoon butter
- 1 package (8 ounces) cream cheese, cubed
- 1 cup sour cream
- 1/2 cup half-and-half cream
- 1/3 cup plus 3 tablespoons grated Parmesan cheese, divided
- 3 garlic cloves, minced
- 1/8 teaspoon pepper
- 2 cans (14 ounces each) water-packed artichoke hearts, rinsed, drained and chopped
- 1 tablespoon snipped fresh dill
- 1/4 teaspoon seasoned salt
- 8 butter-flavored crackers, coarsely crushed

Direction:

1. Preheat oven to 350. Place half of the spinach in a steamer basket; place in a large saucepan over 1 in. of water. Bring to a boil; cover and steam for 3-4 minutes or just until wilted. Transfer to a large bowl.
2. Repeat with remaining spinach; set aside., In a large saucepan, saute onion in butter until tender. Reduce heat to low; stir in the cream cheese, sour cream, half-and-half, 1/3 cup Parmesan cheese, garlic and pepper. Cook and stir until cream cheese is melted. Stir in the artichokes, dill, seasoned salt and spinach.
3. Transfer to an ungreased 2-qt. baking dish. Sprinkle with cracker crumbs and remaining Parmesan cheese. Bake, uncovered, for 20-25 minutes or until edges are bubbly.

Nutrition Information:
- Calories: 196 calories
- Total Fat: 14g fat (8g saturated fat)
- Cholesterol: 45mg cholesterol
- Sodium: 394mg sodium
- Total Carbohydrate: 10g carbohydrate (2g sugars)
- Protein: 7g protein.
- Fiber: 2g fiber

Garlic Roasted Broccoli

"Balsamic vinegar's sweet-tart flavor enhances roasted broccoli spears seasoned with garlic. You can conveniently pop this dish into the oven while a beef roast or turkey is resting. Nella Parker, Hersey, Michigan"

Serving: 8 servings. | Ready in: 30 m

Ingredients:
- 2 bunches broccoli, cut into spears
- 1/3 cup olive oil
- 4 garlic cloves, minced
- 1/2 teaspoon salt
- 1/4 teaspoon pepper
- 2 tablespoons balsamic vinegar

Direction:
1. Place broccoli in a greased 15x10x1-in. baking pan. Combine the oil, garlic, salt and pepper; drizzle over broccoli and toss to coat., Bake, uncovered, at 425 for 15-20 minutes or until tender, stirring occasionally. Drizzle with vinegar.

Nutrition Information:
- Calories: 127 calories
- Total Fat: 10g fat (1g saturated fat)
- Cholesterol: 0 cholesterol mg
- Sodium: 190mg sodium

- Total Carbohydrate: 9g carbohydrate (4g sugars)
- Protein: 5g protein.

Cauliflower Au Gratin Gluten Free

"Are you looking for a yummy side dish for the holidays or your every day meal? Try this low carb cauliflower au gratin recipe to make all meals special."

Serving: 18 servings | Ready in: 60 m

Ingredients:
- 14.5 ounces chicken bone broth
- 3/4 cup heavy cream
- 4 cloves garlic (minced)
- 1/2 teaspoon onion powder
- 1/4 teaspoon poultry seasoning (see note)
- 1 teaspoon xanthan gum (or low carb thickener of choice)
- 32 ounces frozen cauliflower florets (or 2 fresh heads cut into florets)
- 16 ounces freshly grated sharp cheddar cheese (divided (or preferred cheese))
- 8 slices no sugar bacon (cooked and chopped)

Direction:
1. Combine broth, heavy cream, garlic, onion powder, poultry seasoning, and xanthan gum in medium saucepan.

2. Cook liquid over medium heat, stirring frequently, until thickened. Remove from heat.
3. Mix the cauliflower, cheese, and sauce together in 9x13 casserole pan.
4. Sprinkle the chopped bacon on top then cover with remaining cheese.
5. Bake in 350°F oven for 50 minutes or until browned and cauliflower is tender.

Nutrition Information:
- Calories: 192 kcal
- Total Fat: 16 g
- Saturated Fat: 8 g
- Cholesterol: 46 mg
- Sodium: 328 mg
- Total Carbohydrate: 3 g
- Protein: 8 g
- Fiber: 1 g
- Sugar: 1 g

Crispy Brussels Sprouts With Pancetta

" Shredded Brussels get a little Italian flair by roasting them with pancetta until perfectly crisp."

Serving: 4 | Ready in: 28 m

Ingredients:
- 2 pounds Brussels Sprouts (shredded)
- 5 ounces pancetta (chopped)
- Olive oil spray
- 1/2 teaspoon salt
- 1/4 teaspoon black pepper

Direction:
1. Preheat oven to 425°F.
2. Add the Brussels sprouts and pancetta to a large baking sheet and mix well.
3. Spray evenly with oil and sprinkle salt and pepper, mix well and spread into an even layer.
4. Roast for 18 minutes until brown and crispy. Serve warm.

Nutrition Information:
- Calories: 245 kcal
- Total Fat: 14 g
- Saturated Fat: 4 g
- Cholesterol: 23 mg

- Sodium: 582 mg
- Total Carbohydrate: 20 g
- Protein: 12 g
- Fiber: 8 g
- Sugar: 4 g

Keto Stuffing Recipe

"Our keto stuffing recipe is going to be a favorite at all of your holiday meals. It is super simple and has all the traditional flavors. If you are looking for a holiday recipe everyone will eat (without making a low carb and regular version) this is it!"

Serving: 4 Servings | Ready in: 20 m

Ingredients:
- 4 Slices Keto Bread (or rolls) (crumbled)
- 3 tbsp Butter (melted)
- 2 stalks Celery (chopped)
- 1/4 cup Leeks (chopped)
- 1/2 tsp Garlic (minced)
- 1 tsp Italian Blend Seasoning (dried)
- 1/4 tsp Sage
- 1/2 tsp each Salt & Pepper
- Olive Oil
- 1/2 tsp Celery Seasoning (optional)
- 1/2 Cup Chicken broth

Direction:

1. Crumble the keto bread, drizzle with olive oil and bake for about 5 minutes until lightly browned.
2. Saute chopped veggies in olive oil for a minute or two to bring out flavors. Mix together with melted butter and chicken broth
3. Bake on 350 covered with foil for 10 minutes and uncovered for 5 minutes. Serve!

Nutrition Information:
- Calories: 128 kcal

Roasted Broccoli And Cauliflower Recipe With Parmesan Garlic Low Carb Glutenfree

"This healthy roasted broccoli and cauliflower recipe with parmesan and garlic is quick and easy with just 5 ingredients. A delicious way to serve veggies!"

Serving: 12 3/4-cup servings | Ready in: 25 m

Ingredients:
- 4 cups Broccoli (florets)
- 4 cups Cauliflower (florets)
- 1/3 cup Olive oil
- 6 cloves Garlic (minced)
- 2/3 cup Grated parmesan cheese (divided)
- Sea salt
- Black pepper

Direction:
1. Preheat the oven to 400 degrees F. Line a large baking sheet (or two smaller ones that can fit side by side) with foil or parchment paper.
2. Mix the broccoli and cauliflower florets in a large bowl. Add the olive oil, garlic, and half of the parmesan cheese. Toss to coat. Sprinkle with sea salt and black pepper, then toss again.

3. Arrange the veggies in a single layer on the lined baking sheet(s), giving them plenty of room to breathe. Bake for 18-22 minutes*, until the edges are browned. (Toss halfway through for more even cooking - optional but works better.)
4. Right before serving, toss with remaining parmesan cheese, and sprinkle with additional salt & pepper to taste if desired.

Nutrition Information:
- Calories: 90 kcal
- Total Fat: 6 g
- Saturated Fat: 1 g
- Cholesterol: 3 mg
- Sodium: 109 mg
- Total Carbohydrate: 6 g
- Protein: 4 g
- Fiber: 3 g
- Sugar: 2 g

Southernstyle Green Beans

"Green Beans cooked low and slow until soft and tender in a bacon-infused broth."

Serving: 6 | Ready in: 75 m

Ingredients:
- 4 slices bacon,, (diced)
- 2 pounds green beans (ends snapped off and longer beans snapped in half)
- 2 cups chicken broth
- 2 cups water
- 1 teaspoon seasoned salt
- 1/2 teaspoon black pepper
- 1/2 teaspoon garlic powder
- 1/4 teaspoon red pepper flakes
- 1 tablespoon butter, (optional)

Direction:
1. Brown and crisp bacon in a large pot. Remove bacon from pot and reserve.
2. Add green beans to pot along with all remaining ingredients, except butter.
3. Bring to a boil and then turn heat to medium-low. Cover and simmer for 1- 2 hours, stirring occasionally.

4. Drain beans and add butter if using. Check beans for seasoning and add extra salt and pepper to taste. I like lots of black pepper. Sprinkle with bacon and toss to distribute the bacon and butter.

Nutrition Information:
- Calories: 134 kcal

Sugar Free Gingerbread Men

"Sugar free gingerbread men are the perfect treat to take to festive parties or why not make them all year round for a crunchy cookie?"

Serving: 30 gingerbread shapes | Ready in: 32 m

Ingredients:
- 110 g butter (softened)
- 4 tbsp granulated sweetener of choice (or more, to your taste)
- 1 egg
- 200 g almond meal/flour
- 4 tbsp coconut flour
- 2 tsp ground ginger
- 1/2 tsp ground cloves
- 4 tbsp butter
- 4 tbsp cream cheese (regular not spreadable)
- powdered sweetener (to taste)
- 1 tsp vanilla

Direction:
5. Mix the butter and sweetener together until light and fluffy.
6. Add the egg and mix.
7. Add all the other dry ingredients and mix until well combined.
8. Adjust the dough with extra almond flour or water until the dough is the right consistency to be rolled out.

9. Roll between two sheets of baking parchment, cut out various shapes using cookie cutters and place on a lined baking tray.
10. Bake at 180C/350F for 10-12 minutes or until cooked (cooking times will vary considerably for this recipe and how crispy you like your gingerbread men). Once cooked, you may want to turn them upside down and bake for a further minute to ensure they are crisp.
11. Microwave for 10-15 seconds or heat on the stove gently to soften (not melt) the butter and cream cheese together. Mix.
12. Add the vanilla and add sweetener to taste. Mix.
13. Allow to cool slightly and thicken enough to be able to be piped onto the gingerbread men.
14. If the icing/frosting is too thick, add a few drops of water, if too thin, allow to cool in the fridge to allow the butter and cream cheese to solidify slightly.

Nutrition Information:
- Calories: 68 kcal
- Total Fat: 6.3 g
- Total Carbohydrate: 2 g
- Protein: 1.8 g
- Fiber: 1 g
- Sugar: 0.3 g

Sugar Free Walnut And Brandy Truffles

"Sugar free walnut and brandy truffles are so filling, you may only be able to eat one (or possibly two) but that's the point. High healthy fats keep you fuller for longer, and keeps those high sugar treats craving away."

Serving: 20 | Ready in: 15 m

Ingredients:
- 250 g cream cheese (not spreadable)
- 110 g butter (melted)
- 4 tbsp cocoa (unsweetened)
- 1/4 cup walnut pieces
- 3 tbsp granulated sweetener of choice (or more, to your taste)
- 2 tbsp brandy see notes

Direction:
1. Warm the cream cheese block to room temperature or in the microwave for 15 seconds, until it is soft enough to work with.
2. Add the melted butter and mix through with a fork to ensure it is lump free and smooth.
3. Add the cocoa powder, sweetener and brandy. Mix until thoroughly mbined.
4. Gently stir through the tiny walnut pieces and refrigerate until firm enough to roll into balls.

5. Roll a heaped teaspoon at a time and place each truffle on a plate. Place the plate into the fridge again for an hour or two for the truffles to really set firmly.
6. Roll in cocoa powder if you like, or crushed walnuts, pistachios, pecans etc.

Nutrition Information:
- Calories: 94 kcal
- Total Fat: 9.6 g
- Total Carbohydrate: 1.3 g
- Protein: 1.4 g
- Fiber: 0.5 g

Chicken Mole

"If you're not familiar with mole (pronounced mo-LAY), don't be afraid of this versatile Mexican sauce. I love sharing this chicken mole recipe because it's a great one to experiment with. Darlene Morris, Franklinton, Louisiana"

Serving: 12 servings. | Ready in: 06 h 25 m

Ingredients:
- 12 bone-in chicken thighs (about 4-1/2 pounds), skin removed
- 1 teaspoon salt
- MOLE SAUCE:
- 1 can (28 ounces) whole tomatoes, drained
- 1 medium onion, chopped
- 2 dried ancho chilies, stems and seeds removed
- 1/2 cup sliced almonds, toasted
- 1/4 cup raisins
- 3 ounces bittersweet chocolate, chopped
- 3 tablespoons olive oil
- 1 chipotle pepper in adobo sauce
- 3 garlic cloves, peeled and halved
- 3/4 teaspoon ground cumin
- 1/2 teaspoon ground cinnamon
- Fresh cilantro leaves, optional

Direction:

1. Sprinkle chicken with salt; place in a 5- or 6-qt. slow cooker. Place the tomatoes, onion, chilies, almonds, raisins, chocolate, oil, chipotle pepper, garlic, cumin and cinnamon in a food processor; cover and process until blended. Pour over chicken.
2. Cover and cook on low for 6-8 hours or until chicken is tender; skim fat. Serve chicken with sauce, and sprinkle with cilantro if desired. Freeze option: Cool chicken in mole sauce.
3. Freeze in freezer containers. To use, partially thaw in refrigerator overnight. Heat through slowly in a covered skillet or Dutch oven until a thermometer inserted in chicken reads 165, stirring occasionally and adding a little broth or water if necessary.

Nutrition Information:
- Calories: 311 calories
- Total Fat: 18g fat (5g saturated fat)
- Cholesterol: 86mg cholesterol
- Sodium: 378mg sodium
- Total Carbohydrate: 12g carbohydrate (7g sugars)
- Protein: 26g protein.
- Fiber: 3g fiber

Classic Gingerbread Men Low Carb And Gluten Free

"Classic Gingerbread Men cookies made low carb and gluten-free. Perfect for decorating with your kids and giving as a healthy holiday gift."

Ingredients:
- 4 cups almond flour (Honeyville)
- 1 cup Swerve Sweetener
- 1/4 cup Coconut flour
- 2 tbsp ground ginger
- 1 tbsp ground cinnamon
- 2 tsp baking powder
- 1 tsp xanthan gum
- 1/2 tsp salt
- 1/2 tsp ground cloves
- 2 large eggs
- 1/4 cup Kelapo coconut oil (melted)
- 3 tbsp molasses
- 1 tsp vanilla extract
- 1/2 lb powdered Swerve Sweetener
- 1 ½ tbsp meringue powder
- 1 ½ tsp arrowroot starch OR 1/8 tsp xanthan gum

- 1/4 cup lukewarm water (more if needed to thin out)

Direction:

1. For the cookies, preheat oven to 275F and line two baking sheets with parchment paper.
2. In a large bowl, whisk together almond flour, sweetener, coconut flour, ginger, cinnamon, baking powder, xanthan gum, salt and cloves.
3. Stir in eggs, coconut oil, molasses and vanilla extract until dough comes together.
4. Divide dough in half and turn out first half onto a large piece of parchment paper. Top with another piece of parchment and roll out out about 1/4 inch thick.
5. Use cookie cutters to cut into desired shapes and gently loosen and lift with an offset spatula. Place onto prepared baking sheets.
6. Gather up scraps and reroll until too little is left to roll out. Repeat with second half of dough.
7. Bake 20 minutes or until golden brown and just firm to the touch. Remove and let cool 5 minutes on pan, then transfer to a wire rack to cool completely.
8. For the royal icing, in a medium bowl, whisk together powdered sweetener, meringue powder and arrowroot starch or xanthan gum.
9. Add water and stir until smooth. Add more water 1 teaspoon at a time until desired consistency is achieved.
10. Pipe icing onto cooled cookies and let set 30 minutes or longer.
11. For crisper cookies, bake at 225F for 50 to 60 minutes. Remove from oven and let cool. They will crisp up as they cool

Four Ingredient Flourless Sugar Free Pistachio Cookies

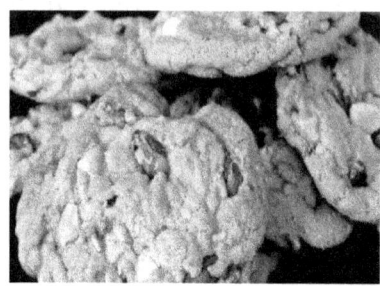

"These Four-Ingredient Flourless, Sugar-Free Pistachio Cookies are one of my favorite healthy little cookies for the holidays."

Serving: 40-50 small cookies | Ready in: 42-45 m

Ingredients:

- 3/4 cup (4 oz.) shelled pistachio nuts, plus about 50 nuts to garnish top of cookies (I used dry-roasted pistachio kernels from Costco)
- 2 T plus 1 cup Splenda or Stevia-in-the-Raw Granulated Sweetener (or use a blend of Splenda/Stevia and sugar or all sugar if you prefer and don't care if it's sugar free)
- 1 2/3 cup almond meal or almond flour
- 2 eggs, beaten well

Direction:

1. In food processor or bowl of immersion blender, combine pistachios with 2 T Splenda or Stevia-in-the-Raw Granulated Sweetener and process until the nuts are finely ground.
2. If using food processor change to plastic blade, or transfer pistachio/sweetener mixture to stand mixer fitted with paddle attachment. Add the almond meal or almond flour and

cup of sweetener and mix until well combined. Then add eggs and mix until completely blended into dry ingredients.

3. Remove mixture from food process or mixer bowl and chill at least 8 hours. (I chilled it overnight and baked the cookies the next day.) Preheat the oven to 325F. Line cookie sheet with parchment paper. Scoop a small

spoonfuls of dough and roll between your hands to make a small ball about an inch in diameter. (I used a teaspoon measuring spoon to scoop out the dough.)

4. Put each ball on the parchment, smash down slightly, then press one pistachio into the center. Bake cookies until they are lightly browned on the edges, about 12-15 minutes in my toaster oven. Let cool for 5 minutes on cookie sheet, then transfer to cooling rack or dish towel and let cool.

Glutenfree Low Carb Peanut Butter Cookies Made With Six Ingredients

"These Six Ingredient Peanut Butter Chocolate Chip Cookies are so easy a 10 year old can make them. They're also low carb, gluten-free, dairy-free, keto and terrific! 2 net carbs per cookie."

Serving: 26 cookies | Ready in: 20 m

Ingredients:
- 1 cup Skippy Natural Creamy Peanut Butter
- 1/3 cup Sukrin Gold packed (or Swerve Granulated)
- 1 tablespoon Sukrin Fiber Syrup Gold (or 2 teaspoons of honey - optional but helps with texture and browning)
- 1/2 teaspoon baking soda
- 1 large egg, (cold)
- 1/3 cup Lily's Chocolate Chips (or your favorite sf or low sugar chocolate chips)

Direction:
1. Preheat oven to 350 and place the rack in the middle of the oven.
2. Line a baking sheet with parchment.
3. Put the first 5 ingredients in a medium bowl and mix thoroughly with hand mixer. Add the chocolate chips and mix again.

4. Weigh 1/2 ounce portions of dough, rolling them into a ball and placing 12 on a cookie sheet at a time. Push down with a fork in one direction and then the opposite direction, making the characteristic peanut butter cookie impressions.Bake for 8-10 minutes until the bottoms begin to brown. Let the peanut butter cookies cool for 5 minutes on the baking sheet before moving to a cooling rack to cool completely.
5. Make sure to keep the dough in the refrigerator between batches. This batter performs best when it is cold! Store cookies in the fridge.

Nutrition Information:
- Calories: 64 kcal
- Total Fat: 5 g
- Total Carbohydrate: 3 g
- Protein: 2 g
- Fiber: 1 g

Holiday Praline No Bake Cookies THMS Low Carb Sugar Free

Serving: 12 -13 cookies | Ready in: 15 m
  Ingredients:
- 1/2 Cup Heavy Whipping Cream
- 4 Tablespoons Unsalted Butter
- 1/2 Cup Xylitol (or the equivalent of your favorite sweetener)
- 1 Tablespoon Coconut Oil
- 1 Teaspoon Vanilla Extract
- 1 Cup Unsweetened Shredded Coconut (you want finely shredded, not the large flakes)
- 1 Cup Chopped Pecans
  Direction:
1. In a large saucepan, melt Heavy Whipping Cream, Butter, Xylitol and Coconut Oil.
2. Bring to a low boil and simmer for 10 minutes.
3. Remove from heat and add Vanilla, Shredded Coconut, and Chopped Pecans.

4. Scoop onto a parchment lined cookie sheet, and chill in freezer until firmly set.

Low Carb Peanut Butter Blossoms

Serving: 20 | Ready in: 20 m

Ingredients:
- 4 tbsp Horizon Salted Butter
- 1 cup unsweetened (natural peanut butter)
- 1 tsp vanilla extract
- 1 tspvanilla liquid stevia
- 1/2 cup Swerve confectioners sweetener
- 1 Horizon Egg (beaten)
- 4 ounces sugar-free chocolate chips (I used Lily's Sweets)
- 2 tbsp Horizon salted butter

Direction:
1. Preheat oven to 350 degrees.
2. In a microwavable bowl or in a small bowl set over simmering water, melt the butter and peanut butter together. Stir until smooth.
3. Stir in the vanilla extract, stevia, and Swerve until smooth.
4. Mix in the egg and stir until smooth.
5. Use a tablespoon to measure out 20 cookies and place them onto a parchment lined baking sheet.
6. Use a rounded 1/4 tsp and push the bottom of the teaspoon in the center of each cookie.

7. Bake for 10 minutes.
8. Remove from oven and use the teaspoon again to the center of each cookie.
9. Allow to cool completely.
10. Once cooled, melt chocolate chips and butter together, stir until smooth. Mine took 1 minute in microwave.
11. Spoon chocolate into the center of each cookie. Allow to set or refrigerate for 30 minutes.
12. Enjoy!

Nutrition Information:
- Calories: 132 kcal
- Total Fat: 11.5 g
- Saturated Fat: 4 g
- Cholesterol: 18 mg
- Sodium: 61 mg
- Total Carbohydrate: 6.1 g
- Protein: 3.9 g
- Fiber: 2 g

Peanut Butter Chocolate Chip Cookies Thms Low Carb Sugar Free

Ingredients:
- 1/2 Cup Softened Butter
- 1/4 Cup Natural No Sugar Added Peanut Butter
- 1/3 Cup Low Carb Brown Sugar (I use this one)
- 1/3 Cup Erythritol
- 2 Eggs
- 1/2 Teaspoon Baking Soda
- 1/2 Teaspoon Mineral Salt
- 1 Teaspoon Vanilla Extract
- 1 Cup THM Baking Blend
- 1/2 Cup Lily's Chocolate Chips

Direction:
1. Preheat oven to 350F
2. Cream shortening, "brown sugar" and Erithyritol until smooth.
3. Add peanut butter and beat well.
4. Add eggs and beat well.
5. Add baking soda, mineral salt, vanilla and Baking Blend and beat until incorporated.
6. Stir in chocolate chips.

7. Using a Cookie Scoop, place dough on parchment lined cookie sheet and bake for 10-11 minutes.

Sugar Free Paleo Pecan Snowball Cookies

Serving: 24 | Ready in: 20 m
Ingredients:
- 8 tbsp Ghee (or use butter if not paleo)
- 1 1/2 cup almond flour (150 grams)
- 1 cup pecans (120 grams, chopped)
- 1/2 cup Swerve Confectioners Sweetener (78 grams)
- 1 tsp vanilla extract
- 1/2 tsp vanilla liquid stevia
- 1/4 tsp salt
- extra confectioners to roll balls in

Direction:
1. Preheat oven to 350 degrees F.
2. Place all ingredients into food processor and process until batter forms a ball. Pulse if needed.
3. Taste batter, adjust sweetener if needed.
4. Line a baking sheet with silpat or parchment.
5. Use a cookie scoop and make 24 mounds.
6. Roll each mound in the palm of your hand.
7. Place in freezer for 20-30 minutes.
8. Place in oven for 15 minutes or until golden around edges.
9. Allow to cool slightly.

10. Once able to handle roll each in some confectioners sweetener.
11. Allow to cool completely before storing in an air tight container.

Nutrition Information:
- Calories: 112 kcal
- Total Fat: 11 g
- Saturated Fat: 3 g
- Cholesterol: 12 mg
- Sodium: 24 mg
- Total Carbohydrate: 2 g
- Protein: 1 g
- Fiber: 1 g

Cranberry Glazed Ham Low Carb And Gluten Free

"Looking for a less sugary glaze for your holiday ham? Try this low carb cranberry glaze and sauce, a tart complement to the smoky ham"

Ingredients:
- 1, 4-6 lb Smithfield fully cooked spiral ham
- 12 ounces fresh cranberries
- 1 cup water
- 1/2 cup red wine
- 1/2 cup Swerve Sweetener
- 1 tbsp Dijon mustard

Direction:
1. Preheat oven to 325F and line a large roasting pan with foil. Remove packaging from ham, reserving as much liquid as possible.
2. Place ham, cut-side down, onto foil in roasting pan. Pour reserved liquid over and wrap in foil.
3. Warm ham in oven for 10 minutes per pound.
4. Meanwhile, combine cranberries, water, wine and sweetener in a medium saucepan. Bring to just a boil, then simmer on

medium-low until all of the cranberries have popped, about 10 minutes. Stir in Dijon mustard.
5. Remove ham from oven and remove foil. Spread about half of the cranberry mixture all over ham and return to oven for another 20 minutes.
6. Slice and serve with remaining cranberry sauce.

Ham Gruyere Mini Quiches

"When you make this in muffin cups, each person gets a quiche. I have also doubled the recipe and used jumbo muffin cups; bake about 10 minutes longer. Gena Stout, Ravenden, Arkansas"

Serving: 10 mini quiches. | Ready in: 50 m

Ingredients:
- 4 large Nellie's Free Range Eggs, lightly beaten
- 1 cup 2% cottage cheese
- 1/4 cup 2% milk
- 2 tablespoons all-purpose flour
- 1/2 teaspoon baking powder
- 1/4 teaspoon ground nutmeg
- 1/4 teaspoon pepper
- 1-1/2 cups shredded Gruyere or Swiss cheese
- 3/4 cup finely chopped fully cooked ham
- 3 tablespoons thinly sliced green onions

Direction:
1. Preheat oven to 375degrees. In a large bowl, combine the first seven ingredients; fold in Gruyere cheese, ham and onions. Fill greased muffin cups three-fourths full., Bake 18-22 minutes or until a knife inserted in the center comes out

clean. Cool 5 minutes before removing from pans to wire racks. Freeze option:Bake and cool quiches. Transfer quiches to a large resealable plastic freezer bag and freeze up to 3 months. To use, thaw in the refrigerator overnight. Preheat oven to 350. Transfer quiches to a greased baking sheet; bake 10-14 minutes or until heated through.

Nutrition Information:
- Calories: 144 calories
- Total Fat: 9g fat (5g saturated fat)
- Cholesterol: 112mg cholesterol
- Sodium: 323mg sodium
- Total Carbohydrate: 3g carbohydrate (1g sugars)
- Protein: 12g protein.
- Fiber: 0 fiber g

Baked Parmesan Zucchini Rounds

"A simple summer side dish of Baked Parmesan Zucchini Rounds comes together quickly using only two ingredients...and will disappear from the table even faster!"

Serving: 2 to 4 servings

Ingredients:
- 2 medium-sized zucchini
- 1/2 cup freshly grated Parmesan cheese
- Garlic salt & freshly ground black pepper, optional

Direction:
1. Place oven rack in center position of oven. Preheat to 425°F. Line a baking sheet with foil (lightly misted with cooking spray) OR parchment paper.
2. Wash and dry zucchini, and cut into 1/4-inch thick slices. Arrange zucchini rounds on prepared pan, with little to no space between them. If desired, lightly sprinkle zucchini with garlic salt and freshly ground black pepper. Use a small spoon to spread a thin layer of Parmesan cheese on each slice of zucchini.
3. Bake for 15 to 20 minutes, or until Parmesan turns a light golden brown. (Watch these closely the first time you make them and pull them out of the oven early if the Parmesan is golden before 15 minutes!) Serve immediately.

Buttery Cauliflower Rice Pilaf Low Carb Gluten Free

Serving: 6 cups

Ingredients:
- 1/4 cup butter
- 2 tbsp olive oil
- 4 cloves garlic, minced
- 6 oz onion, diced (about 1 1/2 cups)
- sea salt and black pepper, to taste
- 6 cups riced cauliflower
- 3/4 cup chicken stock
- 1 tbsp powdered chicken granules, more to taste

Direction:
1. Heat butter and olive oil in a large skillet over medium heat. Once melted, add the onion and garlic to the pan. Sprinkle with a little sea salt and black pepper.
2. Sauté until the onions are translucent and the garlic is fragrant.
3. Add the riced cauliflower, chicken stock and powdered chicken granules to the pan. Mix to combine all ingredients.
4. Continue sautéing until all the liquid has evaporated and the cauliflower is completely cooked.

5. Use a rubber spatula to scrape any caramelized bits from the bottom of the pan and mix in. Add additional salt and pepper if needed.

Low Carb Lemon Cheesecake Bars

"A variation of this recipe was in the Woman's World Magazine. Since I am trying to monitor carbs and yet still enjoy dessert, this really fills the bill."

Serving: 8 serving(s) | Ready in: 5 m

Ingredients:
- 1 (3 ounce) package sugar-free lemon gelatin
- 2 tablespoons lemon juice
- 2 (8 ounce) packages low-fat cream cheese
- 1 cup boiling water

Direction:
1. Stir the boiling water into the box of jello, mixing for about 2 minute.
2. Add the cream cheese and lemon juice.
3. Mix until all lumps have disappeared.
4. Pour into an 8" square pan and chill until set.
5. Cut into 8 squares.

Nutrition Information:
- Calories: 181.2
- Total Fat: 12.9 g
- Saturated Fat: 7.3 g
- Cholesterol: 42 mg

- Sodium: 207.4 mg
- Total Carbohydrate: 5.8 g
- Protein: 11.1 g
- Fiber: 0 g
- Sugar: 1.9 g

No Carb Peanut Butter Cookies

"Since I have been on South Beach I have craved a little sweet at night and these fit the bill very nicely and fit in with my plan. The crumble VERY easily so let them cool a bit before taking off the cookie sheet."

Serving: about 4 if 3 cookies each | Ready in: 15 m

Ingredients:
- 1 c natural peanut butter (or your choice)
- 1 large egg
- 1/2 c splenda
- dash vanilla (optional)

Direction:
1. Preheat oven to 350.
2. Mix all the ingredients together. You can add or decrease the Splenda to your own taste.
3. Break off about 12 pieces and roll into a ball the place on a cookie sheet sprayed with Pam. Press down with a fork in the familiar fork patern.
4. Bake for about 10 minutes or until they have stiffened up. Its kind of hard to tell but they will be firm to the touch. Cool then take off the cookie sheet and enjoy. Not your normal

Rosemary Mustard Crusted Baked Ham Low Carb Gluten Free

Ingredients:
- 1 cup prepared mustard
- 1/2 cup mayonnaise
- 2 Tbsp garlic, minced
- 2 Tbsp rosemary, chopped
- freshly ground pepper
- 1 smoked ham

Direction:
1. Combine all ingredients in a small bowl.
2. Place your ham in a roasting pan fat side up. Slather generously with your mustard mixture. Pour about 1/2 cup of water into the bottom of the pan and place in a preheated 300 degree oven. Bake for about 15 minutes per lb. uncovered.
3. Serve with your choice of low carb side dishes - roasted asparagus and some cauli mash would go perfectly! Hope you like it!

Keto Pumpkin Butter Cookies Recipe

Ingredients:
- 2 Cups Almond Flour
- 1/2 Cup Pure Pumpkin
- 1 Large Egg
- 1/2 cup Butter
- 1 tsp Pure Vanilla Extract
- 1/2 tsp Baking Powder
- 1/2 tsp Pumpkin Pie Spice
- 1 tsp Liquid Stevia OR 1/8 tsp Stevia Powder OR 1/2 cup Stevia in the Raw, Splenda, or other Sweetener (add carbs for these)

Direction:
1. Preheat oven to 300
2. Add all ingredients to a mixing bowl and mix until well combined.
3. Roll into 27 balls and place on a greased cookie sheet. Using a fork press dough down lightly.
4. Bake for 20-23 minutes.
5. Allow to cool for 5 minutes.

Nutrition Information:
- Calories: 255 kcal

- Total Fat: 1 g
- Saturated Fat: 0 g
- Cholesterol: 0 mg
- Sodium: 0 mg
- Total Carbohydrate: 51 g
- Protein: 8 mg
- Sugar: 0 g

Better Than Potatoes Cheesy Cauliflower Puree Low Carb

"This Keto Cheesy Cauliflower Puree is so thick, creamy, and delicious, you'll never miss mashed potatoes again!"

Serving: 2 cups

Ingredients:
- 1 head of cauliflower
- 2 Tbsp heavy cream
- 1 Tbsp butter
- 2 ounces dubliner or other sharp cheese
- salt and pepper to taste

Direction:
1. Clean and trim the cauliflower, breaking it into medium sized pieces.
2. Place in a microwave safe bowl with 2 Tbsp of cream and 1 Tbsp of butter.
3. Microwave, uncovered, on high for six minutes.
4. Stir to coat cauliflower with cream/butter mixture. Microwave for another six minutes on high.
5. Remove from the microwave and put into a high speed blender or food processor along with the cheese. Puree until smooth.

6. Season with salt and pepper to taste. You can adjust the cream and butter to your preference.

Nutrition Information:
- Calories: 148
- Total Fat: 11g
- Total Carbohydrate: 4g
- Protein: 6g

Low Carb Avgolemeno Greek Chicken Lemon Egg Soup

Serving: 8 servings

Ingredients:
- 4 cups cooked, shredded chicken
- 10 cups chicken stock or broth
- 3 eggs
- 1/3 cup fresh lemon juice
- 2 cups cooked spaghetti squash
- 1/4 cup fresh parsley, chopped
- salt and pepper to taste
- freshly grated parmesan cheese (optional)

Direction:
1. Add the chicken and broth to a large saucepan and bring to a boil. Remove from the heat. In a medium bowl whisk the eggs and lemon juice together until frothy.
2. Slowly whisk 2 cups of hot stock into the egg mixture - don't just dump it in or you'll end up with scrambled eggs!
3. Once the stock has been incorporated into the egg mixture, add back to the pot.
4. Stir in the spaghetti squash and gently reheat the soup if necessary - don't bring to a boil or the eggs may curdle.

5. Season with salt and pepper.
6. Serve hot, garnished with chopped parsley and grated parmesan cheese (optional).

Low Carb Buffalo Chicken Meatballs

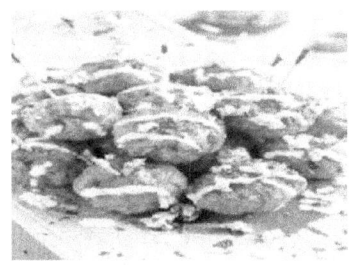

"Please note: The baking temperature of 500 degrees is correct. Please be careful with parchment paper at such a high heat as a few people have commented that their's nearly caught fire. Be sure none is overhanging your pan or just lightly spray your pan with non-stick spray and skip the parchment altogether."

Serving: 9 meabtalls | Ready in: 20 m

Ingredients:
- 1 pound ground chicken or turkey
- 1/2 cup almond flour
- 1/4 cup grated cheddar cheese
- 2 tablespooons prepared ranch dressing (plus more for serving)
- 1 tablespoon dry ranch seasoning
- 1/4 cup hot sauce (plus more for serving)
- 1 egg

Direction:
1. Preheat oven to 500 degrees. Line baking sheet with parchment paper.
2. Add all of the ingredients to a medium bowl and mix well with your hands.
3. Form mixture into 9 evenly sized meatballs and place on the prepared baking sheet.

4. Bake for 15 minutes or until cooked through.
5. erve with extra hot sauce and ranch dressing, as desired

Nutrition Information:
- Calories: 156 kcal
- Total Fat: 11 g
- Total Carbohydrate: 2 g
- Protein: 12 g
- Fiber: 1 g

Low Carb Cheese Crackers Recipe Keto Friendly

Serving: 30 -35 | Ready in: 30 m

Ingredients:
- 2 Cups Cheese of your choice (I used a Parmesan-Romano mix along with some swiss and cheddar)
- 1 cup Almond Flour
- 2 oz Cream Cheese
- 1 egg
- 1/2 teaspoon sea salt
- 1 teaspoon Rosemary (or a seasoning of your choice such as basil, chives, garlic, dill weed, spicy chili etc...)

Direction:
1. Mix all the cheeses (including the cream cheese) along with the almond flour in a microwave safe bowl and cook it for exactly one minute.
2. Immediately stir the ingredients until the almond flour and cheeses have combined fully. You want the cheese to be partially melted (see photo)
3. Allow this to cool for a few minutes because if you put the egg in these ingredients too soon it will cook the egg.
4. Now add the egg, sea salt and seasoning of your choice. I decided to cut up some fresh rosemary I had on hand. You

want to add about a teaspoon of your favorite seasoning unless it's a spicy mix. I would add only about a 1/2 teaspoon for spicy seasonings.
5. Mix it together until all the ingredients is fully combined. If you cheese has gotten too hard or it's too hard to mix, you can microwave your cheese for another 20 seconds to get it soft again.
6. Now you will place the ball of dough on a large sheet of parchment paper. Then place another sheet of parchment paper of equal size on top of the ball of dough.
7. You can use your hands or a rolling pin to spread the dough out into a thin layer. It spread so easily that I used my hands to have more control and keep the dough inside the square piece of parchment paper. Make sure the parchment paper is the same size as your baking sheet.
8. Next use a pizza cutter to cut the crackers into small squares as seen in the photos.
9. Bake these crackers on each side at 450 degrees for about 5 or 6 minutes on each side. If the crackers are thin, you will cook them about 5 minutes on each side but if the dough is thick, it may take 7 to 9 minutes to get the crispy cracker texture you are looking for. When you keep the dough on the parchment paper it's really easy to flip it over while it's hot after cooking it on the first side. I ended up using the pizza cutter again to define the lines on the flip side too. Feel free to leave the crackers in there a bit longer (but watch them closely) if you love a very crispy texture.
10. Allow the crackers to cool for about 5 minutes and they are

Low Carb Pumpkin Cheesecake Mousse

Serving: 12 | Ready in: 5 m

Ingredients:
- 16 ounces cream cheese (room temp)
- 15 ounce canned pumpkin (not pumpkin pie filling)
- 2 cups heavy cream
- 1/4 tsp salt
- 2 teaspoons pumpkin pie spice (or use cinnamon, ginger, nutmeg, cloves)
- 1-2 teaspoons Pumpkin Spice liquid stevia or Vanilla Stevia to taste
- 1 teaspoon vanilla extract
- Optional toppings: Sukrin Gold Brown Sugar Substitute

Direction:
1. In a KitchenAid or stand mixer blend cream cheese and pumpkin until smooth.
2. Add the rest of the ingredients and blend until whipped and fluffy about 5 minutes.
3. Taste and adjust sweetener to your liking if needed.

4. Pipe into serving glasses and top with cacao nibs or brown sugar sub like Sukrin if desired. Best if Chilled about an hour to set and thicken but still fantastic to enjoy immediately!
5. Keep refrigerated until ready to serve.

Nutrition Information:
- Calories: 280 kcal
- Total Fat: 27 g
- Saturated Fat: 16 g
- Cholesterol: 95 mg
- Sodium: 186 mg
- Total Carbohydrate: 5 g
- Protein: 3 g
- Fiber: 1 g
- Sugar: 2 g

Oven Roasted Green Beans

Ingredients:

"Oven Roasted Green Beans" Serving: 4 | Ready in: 30 m

- 1 pound of frozen green beans
- 2 tablespoons olive oil
- 1/2 teaspoon salt
- About 10 grinds of fresh ground pepper (or to taste)
- 1/2 teaspoon onion powder
- 1/2 teaspoon garlic powder

Direction:
1. Preheat oven to 425 degrees
2. Prepare a lipped baking sheet with aluminum foil
3. In a medium bowl combine all ingredients and toss
4. Spread beans onto baking sheet
5. Roast for 30 minutes (at 15 minute remove to stir)
6. Serve immediately

Parmesan Roasted Tomatoes Recipe

"Parmesan Roasted Tomatoes - juicy and plump roasted tomatoes loaded with Parmesan cheese. So easy to make, fool-proof and amazing!"

Serving: 6 | Ready in: 25 m

Ingredients:
- 6 small tomatoes (halved)
- 1 tablespoon olive oil
- Pinch of salt
- Ground black pepper
- 1/2 cup grated Parmesan cheese

Direction:

1. Preheat the oven to 400F.

2. Rinse the tomatoes and sliced into halves. Toss gently with the olive oil. Season with salt and pepper. Arrange the tomatoes on a baking dish, and top with Parmesan cheese. Roast the tomatoes for about 15-20 minutes or until the Parmesan cheese melted and the top is slightly browned.

3. Remove from the oven and serve immediately.

Nutrition Information:
- Calories: 111 kcal
- Total Fat: 7.5 g

- Saturated Fat: 3.7 g
- Cholesterol: 17 mg
- Sodium: 248 mg
- Total Carbohydrate: 4.4 g
- Protein: 8.3 g
- Fiber: 1.1 g

Keto Brownies With Peppermint Crunch

"Don't stress out about your upcoming holiday parties. These delicious keto brownies with peppermint crunch will satisfy any group of holiday guests!"

Serving: 8 brownies | Ready in: 40 m

Ingredients:
- 1 4oz low carb chocolate bar (Lily's Stevia Sweetened Baking Bar)
- 1/3 cup coconut oil or softened butter
- 4 large eggs
- 1/4 scant cup coconut flour
- 1/4 cup cacao powder
- 2 tablespoons erythritol or xylitol
- 1 teaspoon baking powder
- 1/4 teaspoon salt
- 1/4 cup chopped pili nuts or pecans
- 1 teaspoon peppermint extract
- 1 teaspoon erythritol or xylitol
- 1 teaspoon Ceylon cinnamon

Direction:
1. You will need a small loaf pan (8x4) and parchment paper.
2. Line the loaf pan with parchment paper, and pre-heat the oven to 350F.

3. Chop up the chocolate and combine half of it with the coconut oil. Set the rest aside.
4. Microwave the chocolate and coconut oil for 30 seconds to melt. Stir until smooth.
5. Crack the eggs into a medium bowl, slowly pour in the melted chocolate mix while you whisk the eggs until thick and combined. Doesn't have to be totally smooth. Use a spatula to scrape any left-over chocolate in there.
6. Whisk together the dry ingredients into a separate bowl then add in the wet mix and use a spatula to fold it all together until the batter is thick and dark brown. Fold in the rest of the chopped chocolate.
7. Use the spatula to scrape all of the batter into the loaf pan and smooth it out.
8. Chop up the nuts and mix in a small bowl with the cinnamon, sweetener and peppermint. Then spoon it over the brownie batter.
9. Place in the center rack and bake for 30 minutes or until a toothpick comes out almost clean when inserted in the center.
10. Remove from the oven and let it cool. Lift up the brownie by the parchment paper and place on a cutting board. Cut in to 8 even squares.

Nutrition Information:
- Calories: 205
- Total Fat: 18g
- Total Carbohydrate: 15g
- Protein: 5g
- Fiber: 9g
- Sugar: Sugar Alcohols 3g

Spicy Broccoli With Garlic

"Garlic and spiced crushed red pepper add kick and spice to broccoli." Serving: 4 servings | Ready in: P0DT0 h 10 m

Ingredients:
- 1 1/2 pounds broccoli
- 4 1/2 tablespoons olive oil
- 1 clove garlic, minced
- 1/4 teaspoon salt
- 1/8 teaspoon crushed red pepper
- 1 1/2 teaspoons vinegar
- 3/4 cup water

Direction:
1. Peel and slice thick stems from broccoli; separate florets.
2. In a skillet, bring water to a simmer over medium-low heat. Add stems and florets; cook, covered, until bright green, 4 minutes.
3. Stir in olive oil, minced garlic, salt, and crushed red pepper. Cook 4 minutes.
4. Turn off heat; stir in vinegar.

Low Carb White Chocolate Coconut Fudge Paleo Keto

Serving: 24 pieces | Ready in: 10 m

Ingredients:
- 4 ounces cacao butter
- 15 ounces coconut milk
- 1/2 cup coconut oil
- 1 cup coconut butter
- 1/2 cup vanilla egg white protein powder (Jay Robbs brand)
- 1 teaspoon vanilla extract
- 1 teaspoon coconut liquid stevia
- pinch salt
- Optional topping: unsweetened coconut flakes

Direction:
1. Melt the cacao butter in a sauce pan over low heat.
2. Stir in the coconut milk, coconut oil and coconut butter.
3. Continue to stir until completely smooth, no lumps.
4. Turn off heat and whisk is protein powder, vanilla extract, stevia and salt.
5. Pour mixture into a parchment lined 8 by 8 pan.
6. Sprinkle with coconut flakes if desired.
7. Refrigerate 4 hours or overnight.

8. Does not need to be kept refrigerated for storage.

Nutrition Information:
- Calories: 159 kcal
- Total Fat: 16 g
- Saturated Fat: 10 g
- Sodium: 16 mg
- Total Carbohydrate: 2 g
- Protein: 2 g
- Fiber: 1 g

Cranberry Orange Cardamom Glaze

Ingredients:
- 2 cups water
- 1 cup fresh or frozen cranberries
- zest and juice of one orange
- 5 cardamom pods or 1 tsp ground cardamom
- 2 Tbsp granulated sugar substitute
- 1/4 tsp orange extract
- 1/2 tsp xanthan gum

Direction:
1. In a small saucepan, bring the water, cranberries, orange juice, orange zest, and cardamom to a boil. Simmer for 20 minutes. Mash the cranberries with a fork to release the juice. Stir in sugar substitute until dissolved.
2. Strain out the solids and set aside, removing cardamom pods if using. Add the orange extract and xanthan gum to the liquid and stir until slightly thickened.
3. Brush the liquid onto the duck in the last 15 minutes of roasting (see roasting instructions above.) Stir the solids back into any remaining glaze, and serve it alongside the cooked duck.

Spicy Molasses Cookies Gluten Free Refined Sugarfree

Serving: 30 | Ready in: 20 m

Ingredients:
- 1/2 cup butter (softened)
- 2 teaspoons liquid cinnamon or vanilla stevia
- 1 egg
- 1/2 teaspoon vanilla extract
- 1 1/4 cup gluten free flour
- 1 teaspoon cream of tartar
- 1/2 teaspoon gluten free baking soda
- 1/8 teaspoon salt
- 1 teaspoons ground cinnamon
- 1/2 teaspoon ground nutmeg
- 1/2 teaspoon ground ginger
- 2 tablespoons molasses
- optional: 1/2 cup Enjoy Life chocolate chips
- optional coating: 1 1/2 teaspoon ground cinnamon (2 tablespoons sucanat)

Direction:
1. Preheat oven to 350 degrees.
2. In a stand mixer beat butter, stevia, egg and vanilla extract on medium speed 3 for about 2-3 minutes.

3. Mix in flour, cream of tartar, baking soda and salt until blended.
4. Add in cinnamon, nutmeg, ginger and molasses scraping down the sides of the bowl between mixing as needed.
5. Stir in optional chocolate chips if using.
6. Chill for about 30 minutes in refrigerator if the batter is too soft to roll into balls.
7. Roll into 1 inch balls and place on a parchment lined baking sheet.
8. If using coating, mix ingredients together in a small bowl and roll each ball in coating.
9. Bake 8-10 minutes.
10. Cool for a minute on pan then remove to a wire rack to finish cooling.

Nutrition Information:
- Calories: 71 kcal
- Total Fat: 5 g
- Cholesterol: 15 mg
- Sodium: 57 mg
- Total Carbohydrate: 7 g
- Protein: 1 g
- Fiber: 1 g
- Sugar: 3 g

Pumpkin Pie Snowball Cookies

"Pumpkin Pie Snowball Cookies are snowball cookies with pumpkin pie flavor."

Serving: 15 | Ready in: 31 m

Ingredients:
- 1 ¼ cup almond flour (where to buy almond flour)
- 1 tbsp coconut flour
- 1/3 cup sweetener of choice: coconut sugar for paleo (or for low carb use erythritol granular)
- ½ tbsp pumpkin pie spice
- ¼ tsp cinnamon
- 3 tbsp butter (melted or coconut oil, melted)
- 1 egg yolk (beaten)
- 3 tbsp pumpkin puree (make sure pumpkin is the only ingredient)
- 2 tbsp crushed walnut pieces *optional
- Coating for After Baking
- 2 ½ tbsp . powdered sweetener of choice: grind up coconut sugar in blender or processor (or for low carb use confectioners erythritol or grind up granular erythritol.)
- ½ tsp cinnamon

Direction:

1. Preheat oven to 300 F°, and line or grease a cookie sheet. In a large mixing bowl combine: 1 ¼ cup almond flour, 1 tbsp coconut flour, 1/3 cup sweetener of choice, ½ tbsp. pumpkin pie spice, and ¼ tsp cinnamon. Mix together thoroughly.
2. Add to mixture: 3 tbsp melted butter or coconut oil, 1 egg yolk, and 3 tbsp pumpkin puree. Mix together thoroughly. Add in optional walnut pieces and stir in.
3. In a blender or processor, grind up the 2 ½ tbsp sweetener of choice until it is powdered (unless using a low carb brand of confectioner's sweetener). Put the powdered sweetener of choice into a small to medium size bowl and mix in the ½ tsp cinnamon. Set aside.
4. Using hands or oiled or buttered hands to prevent sticking, roll a tbsp size of pumpkin dough into balls and place on cookie sheet in rows. Bake cookie pie balls in oven for 22 to 26 minutes. Check at 22 minutes to see if browning slightly. Remove from oven and cool slightly.
5. While cookie pie balls are still warm, rolls lightly into the powdered sweetener and cinnamon mixture. Serve and enjoy. Store unused portions in container in the fridge.

Nutrition Information:
- Calories: 81 kcal
- Total Fat: 7 g
- Saturated Fat: 2 g
- Total Carbohydrate: 4 g
- Protein: 2 g

Chocolate Gingerbread Men Grain Free

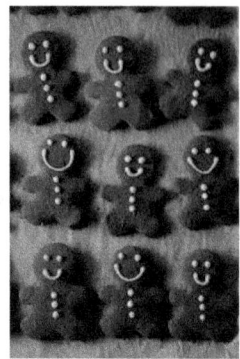

"A fun, paleo, chocolate gingerbread holiday cookie with low carb options."

Serving: 18 | Ready in: 32 m

Ingredients:
- Cookie Ingredients:
- 2/3 cup almond flour (where to buy almond flour)
- 1/3 cup coconut flour (sifted, where to buy coconut flour)
- ¼ cup cocoa or cacao powder (sifted, where to buy cacao powder)
- cup Sweetener of choice: 2/3 coconut sugar for paleo (or 2/3 cup erythritol for low carb, where to buy erythritol)
- 1/2 tsp baking soda (or 1 tsp baking powder)
- 1 1/2 tsp ground ginger spice
- 1 tsp cinnamon
- ¼ tsp nutmeg
- 1/8 tsp sea salt
- 2 eggs (beaten)
- 1/3 cup butter or coconut oil (melted, where to buy coconut oil)
- 2 tbsp organic molasses (where to buy molasses)

- 1 tsp vanilla extract ((organic GF kind), where to buy vanilla extract)
- Paleo Royal Icing * optional:
- 2 tbsp coconut butter (melted, where to buy coconut butter)
- 2 tbsp coconut oil or butter (melted)
- 2 tsp honey or for low carb use 1 1/2 tbsp erythritol (or 1/4 tsp liquid stevia, where to buy liquid stevia)
- 1/8 tsp vanilla extract
- 1/8 tsp lemon juice
- Melted chocolate for decorating *optional:
- 1 ½ tbsp dark chocolate chips (soy and dairy free kind (I use this one) or for low carb use unsweetened chocolate and add sweetener of choice to taste.)

Direction:

1. Preheat oven to 350 F, and line baking sheets with parchment paper.
2. In a large mixing bowl combine: almond flour, coconut flour, cocoa powder, sweetener of choice (coconut sugar or erythritol), baking soda, ground ginger, cinnamon, nutmeg, and sea salt. Mix together thoroughly.
3. In a medium mixing bowl combine: eggs, melted butter or coconut oil, molasses and vanilla extract. Mix together well.
4. Add egg mixture to flour mixture and combine thoroughly.
5. Once dough is thoroughly mixed place bowl of dough in freezer for 8 minutes. Remove from freezer and place between two sheets of parchment paper. Roll dough into a flat rectangle that will fit on your baking sheet.
6. Peel away top parchment paper slowly and place dough on baking sheet.* we are going to bake before cutting with cookie cutters* this is unconventional, but with this kind of dough it works so much better.

7. Bake sheet of dough for 10 to 15 minutes, check at 10 minutes or until browned. Remove baking sheet from oven and let cool for only two

    minutes. Don't remove gingerbread from sheet.
8. Lift parchment paper with gingerbread on it off the baking sheet and onto the counter.
9. Use your cookie cutters now before cookies cool of too much. There will be extra to snack on between cookies. Then place shaped cookies on a plate to cool.
10. Mix all Icing ingredients together and place in a container and put in the fridge for 8 minutes to thicken.
11. Once icing is gel like consistency, then use a small, clean paint brush or butter knife to spread frosting on gingerbread men. Let cookies sit until icing dries (can refrigerate to speed up time).
12. When icing is dry, melt chocolate chips and use a toothpick to draw eyes, mouth, and buttons and to decorate with.
13. Left overs should be stored in a container in the fridge.

Keto Ham Maple Glazed

"Ham is a tradition at Christmas and Easter meals. This keto ham is delicious. It is maple glazed and perfect for Christmas and Easter Lunch or dinner."

Ready in: 60 m

Ingredients:
- 100 ml Sugar Free Maple Syrup (4 fl oz)
- 2 tbsp Tamari or Coconut Aminos
- 2 tbsp Dijon Mustard
- 1 tbsp Worcestershire Sauce
- 1 Whole Leg of Ham, on the bone

Direction:
1. Pre-heat oven to 180 degrees Celsius or 350 Fahrenheit
2. Combine all ingredients for the glaze in a bowl and stir until smooth.
3. Use a small sharp knife to score the skin of the ham around the small hock section. Then slowly peel the skin off by pushing your fingers between the skin and the fat and working your way around. Once the skin is completely removed score the fat with diagonal lines. Just be careful not to score too deep into the meat.
4. Brush the glaze over all the exposed fat on the ham leg and place in the oven for 20 minutes.

5. Remove the ham from the oven and baste with glaze and return to the oven for 10 minutes. Repeat glaze again and put in the oven for a further 10 minutes.
6. Baste for a final time, turn the oven up to 200 degrees celsius (400 Fahrenheit) and cook for a further 5-10 minutes. Keep an eye on it as it may brown quickly.

Low Carb Christmas Tree Platter

"This low carb Christmas tree platter is made from low carb wraps, deli turkey, cream cheese and cranberry sauce!"

Serving: 8 | Ready in: 20 m

Ingredients:
- 4 green low carb wraps
- 4 tbs cream cheese
- 4 turkey slices
- ¼ cup Homemade cranberry sauce (see separate recipe)
- 2 tbs pomegranate seeds (optional)
- 1 thick slice cheese (optional)

Direction:
1. Spread a very thin layer of cream cheese onto a wrap, then add a layer of cooked deli turkey meat.
2. Finish with a thin layer of the cranberry sauce, and roll up the whole wrap.
3. Cut into slices, discard the ends, and start arranging layers of the the sliced wraps onto a plate.
4. To finish, sprinkle some pomegranate seeds over the wraps. Use a star shaped cookie cutter to cut a star from a thick slice of cheese and perch it on the top.

Nutrition Information:
- Calories: 69 kcal
- Total Fat: 3 g
- Saturated Fat: 1 g
- Cholesterol: 11 mg
- Sodium: 122 mg
- Total Carbohydrate: 8 g
- Protein: 4 g
- Fiber: 3 g

Low Carb Cranberry Sauce

"This low carb cranberry sauce is perfect for your festive celebrations! Keto and sugar free recipe."

Serving: 8 | Ready in: 15 m

Ingredients:
- 12 oz fresh cranberries
- ¾ cup water
- ½ cup low carb sweetener (eg xylitol or Swerve)
- ¼ tsp orange extract
- few drops liquid stevia (optional)

Direction:
1. Place the cranberries in a saucepan and remove any that are soft and/or brown.
2. Add the water, sweetener and orange extract. Bring to the boil.
3. Reduce to a medium heat. The cranberries will start bursting and the sauce will form after about 10 minutes. Stir frequently.
4. Add liquid stevia to taste, if required.

Nutrition Information:
- Calories: 19 kcal
- Sodium: 2 mg

- Total Carbohydrate: 4 g
- Fiber: 1 g
- Sugar: 1 g

German Cinnamon Stars Low Carb Christmas Cookies

"It's time to get festive the healthy way: German Cinnamon Stars AKA Zimtsterne are traditional gluten free German Christmas cookies. This version is sugar free and diabetic-friendly."

Serving: 50 stars | Ready in: 45 m

Ingredients:
- 300 g / 3 cups almond flour (ground almonds work well here too)
- 100 g / 1 cup powdered sweetener
- 3 egg whites
- 2 tsp cinnamon
- 1 tsp ground coffee

Direction:
1. Separate the eggs and whip the egg whites until they form stiff peaks. Use a glass or ceramic bowl for this and make sure it's totally dry and squeaky-clean. A stick blender with plastic does not give a brilliant result - best is an old-fashioned mixer with 2 steel attachments.
2. Fold in the sweetener.
3. Reserve 3 tablespoons of the egg white and sugar mix for the glaze

4. Add the almond flour/ground almonds and spices and stir until combined.
5. Form a dough ball and roll it out around 1/2 cam thick between 2 sheets of baking paper
6. Place in the freezer for around 15 minutes. This is an important step - it makes cutting out the dough much easier
7. Remove from the freezer, lift the top baking paper sheet and use a cookie cutter to cut out shapes (just rename the recipe if you prefer hearts instead of stars!)
8. Brush on the egg white mix we set aside earlier.
9. Bake in an pre-heated oven at 120 Celsius for 25 minutes.

Nutrition Information:
- Calories: 34 kcal
- Total Fat: 2.9 g
- Sodium: 2 mg
- Total Carbohydrate: 1.2 g
- Protein: 1.4 g
- Fiber: 0.7 g

The Best Lowcarb Tortilla Chips

"This recipe for the Best Low-Carb Tortilla Chips makes a perfect snack for dipping. Best of all, these chips work for low-carb, Atkins, ketogenic, lc/hf, gluten-free, grain-free, and Banting diets."

Serving: 6 | Ready in: 20 m

Ingredients:
- 2 cups part-skim grated mozzarella cheese
- 3/4 cup super fine almond flour
- 1/2 teaspoon salt
- Optional: 1/2 teaspoon chili powder

Direction:
1. Preheat oven to 375º F. Cut 2 pieces of parchment about 20 inches long. Have a rolling pin and 2 cookie sheets available.
2. Prepare a double boiler. A pot partially filled with water with a mixing bowl that fits on top works well for this purpose. Over high heat, bring the water in the pot to a simmer, then turn heat to low.
3. In the bowl part of the double boiler, add the cheese, almond flour, chili powder (if using), and salt. Using caution to not to get burned by the steam, place the bowl over the pot of simmering water. I use a silicone mitten to hold the bowl. Stir ingredients constantly.

4. As the cheese melts, the ingredients will start to develop a doughy appearance. When it starts to hold together in a ball, turn it out onto a piece of parchment paper.
5. While the dough is hot, but not hot enough to burn your hands, knead the dough to completely mix the ingredients.
6. Divide the dough into 2 equal sections.
7. Form one section into a ball and place on a piece of parchment paper. Pat into a rectangular shape, then cover with another piece of parchment. Using the rolling pin, roll into about a 9 inch by 15 inch rectangle. Dough should be fairly thin. You may need to turn the dough and straighten the parchment if it wrinkles. Remove the top piece of parchment and place the bottom piece of parchment containing the dough on a a cutting board. Using a pizza cutter, cut dough into squares or triangles. Slide the parchment with the triangles onto the cookie sheet. Arrange the triangles of dough so they are at least 1/2 inch away from each other. Set aside.
8. Repeat for the second ball of dough.
9. Place the cookie sheets with the tortilla chips in the oven. Bake for 5-8 minutes or until the centers turn golden brown. Watch them carefully as it is easy to burn them.
10. Remove them from oven and slide them onto a cooling rack using a spatula.
11. Chips will become crunchier as they cool.

Low Carb Cinnamon Chips

"These delicious low carb cinnamon chips are great for a quick snack or tasty dessert!"

Serving: 4 | Ready in: 12 m

Ingredients:
- 4 low carb tortillas
- 1 tsp ground cinnamon
- 1 tsp powdered Swerve (optional)

Direction:
1. Preheat the oven to 350F.
2. Cut the tortillas into 8 wedges and place them in a single layer on baking tray lined with a silicone mat. Sprinkle them with cinnamon and sweetener (if using).
3. Bake for 8-10 minutes or until crispy.

Nutrition Information:
- Calories: 81 kcal
- Total Fat: 2 g
- Saturated Fat: 1 g
- Sodium: 200 mg
- Total Carbohydrate: 13 g
- Protein: 3 g
- Fiber: 10 g

Low Carb Cocoa Nuts

Serving: 6 | Ready in: 62 m
  Ingredients:
- ½ cup pecan halves
- ½ cup walnut halves
- ½ cup slivered almonds
- 2 tbs unsweetened cocoa powder
- 1 tsp vanilla extract
- 2 tsp low carb sweetener (Swerve or similar)
- 2 tbs unsalted butter (melted)
  Direction:
4. Place all the ingredients in a small slow cooker and stir well.
5. Cook on high for 1 hour.
6. Spread the cocoa nuts out onto a baking sheet to cool.
7. Store in an airtight container.

Nutrition Information:
- Calories: 218 kcal
- Total Fat: 21 g
- Saturated Fat: 4 g
- Cholesterol: 10 mg
- Sodium: 1 mg
- Total Carbohydrate: 5 g

- Protein: 4 g
- Fiber: 3 g
- Sugar: 1 g

www.ingramcontent.com/pod-product-compliance
Lightning Source LLC
Chambersburg PA
CBHW071439070526
44578CB00001B/149